THE

TUSCULAN DISPUTATIONS

OF

CICERO.

"O PHILOSOPHY, THOU CONDUCTOR OF LIFE! THOU DISCOVERER OF VIRTUE, AND EXPELLER OF VICES! WHAT HAD NOT ONLY I MYSELF BEEN, BUT THE WHOLE LIFE OF MAN, WITHOUT YOU?"—BOOK V.

OXFORD:

PRINTED BY J. VINCENT.

WHITTAKER AND CO., AVE MARIA LANE;

SIMPKIN AND MARSHALL, STATIONERS' COURT, LONDON.

MDCCCXL.

CONTENTS.

THE

TUSCULAN DISPUTATIONS

OF

MARCUS TULLIUS CICERO.

BOOK I.

ON THE CONTEMPT OF DEATH.

I. As I am, at length, entirely, or to a great degree, freed from the fatigue of defending clients, and the duties of a senator, I have recourse again, BRUTUS, principally by your advice, to those studies which never have been out of my mind, although neglected at times, and which after a long interval I have resumed: and since the reason and precepts of all arts which relate to living well, depend on the study of wisdom, which is called philosophy, I have thought of illustrating this in the Latin tongue; not because philosophy could not be understood in the Greek language, or by Greek masters; but it was always my opinion, that we have been more happy at inventing than the Greeks, or that we have improved on whatever we have received from them, which they have thought worthy their care and pains: for, with regard to manners and economy, family and domestic affairs, we certainly now manage them with more elegance, and better than they did; and our ancestors have, beyond all dispute, formed the republic on better laws and customs. What shall I say of our military affairs; in which, as our ancestors excelled them much in valour, so more in discipline? As to those things which are attained not by study, but nature, neither Greece, nor any nation, is comparable with them; for with whom was ever that gravity, that steadiness, that greatness of soul, probity, faith—such distinguished virtue of every kind, as to equal them with ours? Greece excelled us in learning, and all kinds of literature, and it was easy to do so where there was no competition; for amongst the Greeks the poets were the most ancient species of learned men. Of these Homer and Hesiod were before the foundation of Rome; Archilochus, in the reign of Romulus. We received poetry much later; Livy gives us a fable near five hundred and ten years after the building of Rome, in the consulate of C. Claudius, the son of Cæcus, and M. Tuditanus, a year before the birth of Ennius, who was older than Plautus and Nævius.

II. It was, therefore, late before poets were either known or received amongst us; though we find in Cato de Originibus that the guests used to sing at their entertainments the praises of famous men, to the sound of the flute; but a speech of Cato's shews the custom to have been in no great esteem, as he censures Marcus Nobilior, for carrying poets with him into his province: for that consul, as we know, carried Ennius with him into Ætolia. Therefore the less esteem poets were in, the less were those studies pursued: not but if, had there been amongst us any of great abilities that way, they would not have been at all inferior to the Greeks. Do we imagine that, had it been commendable in Fabius, a man of the first quality, to paint, we should have been without many Polycleti and Parrhasii? Honour nourishes art, and glory is the spur with all to studies; those studies are always neglected, which are a kind of disgrace to any. The Greeks held vocal and instrumental music as the greatest erudition, and therefore it is recorded of Epaminondas, who, in my opinion, was the first man amongst the Greeks, that he played excellently on the flute; and Themistocles some years before was deemed ignorant because he refused at an entertainment to play on the lyre. For this reason musicians flourished in Greece; music was a general study; and whoever was unacquainted with it, was not considered as fully instructed in learning. Geometry was in high esteem with them, therefore none were more honourable than mathematicians: but we have confined this art to bare counting and measuring.

III. But on the contrary, we soon entertained the orator; no ways eloquent at first, but capable enough for an harangue, he soon became eloquent; for it is reported that Galba, Africanus, and Lælius, were men of learning; that even Cato was studious, who was an age before them: then succeeded the Lepidi, Carbo, and Gracchi, and so many great orators after them, even to our times, that we were very little, if at all, inferior to the Greeks. Philosophy has been at a low ebb even to this present time, and had no assistance from our own language, which I have undertaken to raise and illustrate; so that, as I have been of service to my countrymen, when employed in public affairs, I may, if possible, be so to them in my retirement. In this I must take the more pains, because many books are said to be written inaccurately, by excellent men, but not erudite scholars: for indeed it may be that a man may think well, and yet not be able to express his thoughts elegantly; but for any one to publish thoughts which he can neither methodize, nor illustrate nor entertain his reader, is an unpardonable abuse of letters and retirement: they, therefore, read their books to one another, which were never taken up by any but those who claimed the same privilege of writing. Wherefore, if oratory has acquired any reputation from my application to it, I shall, with more pains, open the fountains of philosophy, from which flowed all the advantages of the other. But,

IV. As ARISTOTLE, a man of excellent parts, abundant in all knowledge, being moved at the glory of the rhetorician Isocrates, commenced teacher of youth, and joined philosophy with eloquence: so it is my design not to lay aside my former study of oratory, and yet employ myself in this greater and more fruitful art; for I always thought, that to be able to speak copiously and elegantly on the most important questions, was the most consummate philosophy, to which subject I have so diligently applied myself, that I have already ventured to have Disputations like the Greeks. And lately when you left us, having many of my friends about me, I attempted at my Tusculum what I could do in that way; for as I formerly practised declaiming, which nobody continued longer than myself, so this is now to be the declamation of my old age. I ordered a person to propose something he would have discussed: I disputed on that, either sitting or walking, and have compiled the scholæ as the Greeks call them, of five days, in as many books. It was in this manner: when he who was the hearer had said what he thought proper, I disputed against him; for this is, you know, the old and Socratic method of disputing against another's opinion; for Socrates thought the truth might thus the easier be discovered. But to give you a better notion of our disputations, I will not barely send you an account of them, but represent them to you as they were carried on; therefore let the introduction be thus.

V. *A*. To me death seems to be an evil. *M*. What, to those who are already dead? or to those who must die? *A*. To both. *M*. It is a misery then, because an evil? *A*. Certainly. *M*. Then those who must soon die, and those who must die some time or other, are both miserable? *A*. So it appears to me. *M*. Then all are miserable? *A*. Every one. *M*. And, indeed, if you are consistent with yourself, all that are already born, or shall be, are not only miserable, but always will be so; for should you maintain those only to be miserable, who must die, you would not except any one living, for all must die; but there should be an end of misery in death. But seeing that the dead are miserable, we are born to eternal misery, for they must of consequence be miserable who died a hundred thousand years ago; or rather, all that have been born. *A*. So indeed I think. *M*. Tell me, I beseech you, are you afraid of the three-headed Cerberus below, the roaring waves of Cocytus, the passage over Acheron, Tantalus expiring with thirst, while the water touches his chin; or Sisyphus,

> Who sweats with arduous toil to gain
> The steepy summit of the mount in vain?

Perhaps, too, you dread the inexorable judges, Minos and Rhadamanthus, before whom nor Crassus, nor M. Antonius can defend you; nor, since the cause lies before Grecian judges, Demosthenes. But you must plead for yourself before a very great assembly: you dread perhaps these, and therefore look on death as an eternal evil.

VI. *A*. Do you take me to be mad enough to give credit to such things? *M*. What? do you not believe them? *A*. Not in the least. *M*. I am sorry to hear that. *A*. Why, I beg? *M*. Because I could have been very eloquent in speaking against them. *A*. And who could not on such a subject? or, what occasion is there to refute these monsters of the poets and painters? *M.* And yet you have books of philosophers full of arguments against these. *A.* Idle enough, truly! for, who is so weak as to be concerned about them? *M.* If then there are none miserable in the infernal regions, there must be no one there. *A.* I am altogether of that opinion. *M.* Where then are those you call miserable? or what place do they inhabit? if they are at all, they must be somewhere? *A.* I, indeed, am of opinion, they are nowhere. *M.* Therefore there are none such. *A.* Even so, and yet they are miserable for this very reason, that they are not at all. *M.* I had rather now that you had been afraid of Cerberus, than to speak thus inaccurately. *A.* Why so; *M.* Because you admit him to be, who is not; where is your sagacity? When you say any one is miserable, you say such a one is, when he is not. *A.* I am not so absurd as to say that. *M.* What is it you say then? *A.* I say, for instance, that Crassus is miserable in being deprived of such great riches by death; that Cn. Pompey was so, in being taken from such glory and honour; upon the whole, that all are miserable who are deprived of this light. *M.* You have returned to the same point, for to be miserable implies an existence; but you just now denied that the dead had any existence; if they are not, they can be nothing; and if so, not miserable. *A.* Perhaps I do not express what I mean, for I look upon this very thing, not to exist, after having been, to be very miserable. *M.* What, more so than not to have been at all? therefore, those who are not yet born, are miserable because they are not; and we ourselves, if we are to be miserable after death, were miserable before we were born: but I do not remember I was miserable before I was born; and I should be glad to know, if your memory is better, what you recollect of yourself before you were born.

VII. *A.* You are pleasant; as if I had said, they are miserable who are not born, and that they are not so who are dead. *M.* You say then that they are so? *A.* Yes, because they are most miserable not to be, after they have been. *M.* You do not observe, that you assert contradictions; for what is a greater contradiction, than that that should be not only miserable, but should be at all, which is not? When you go out at the Capene gate and see the tombs of the Calatini, the Scipios, Servilii, and Metelli, do you look on them as miserable? *A.* Because you distress me with a word, henceforward I will not say they are miserable in general, but miserable for this, that they are not. *M.* You do not say then M. Crassus is miserable, but only miserable M. Crassus. *A.* Evidently so. *M.* As if it did not follow, that whatever you declare in that manner, either is or is not. Are you not acquainted with the first principles of logic? for this is the first thing they lay down, whatever is asserted, (for so I render the Greek term, ἀξίωμα, I may express it otherwise when I shall find a better,) is therefore asserted, because it is either true or false. When, therefore, you say miserable M. Crassus, you either say this, that M. Crassus is miserable, so that some judgment may be made whether it be true or false, or you say nothing. *A.* Well then, I now own that the dead are not miserable, since you have drawn from me a concession, that they who are not at all, cannot be miserable. What then? we that are alive, are we not wretched, seeing we must die? for what is there agreeable in life, when we must night and day reflect that we may instantly die?

VIII. *M.* Do you not then perceive how great an

evil you have delivered human nature from? *A.* By what means? *M.* Because, if to die is miserable to the dead, to live would be a kind of infinite and eternal misery: now I see a goal, which when I have reached, there is nothing more to be feared; but you seem to me to follow the opinion of Epicharmus, a man of some discernment, and sharp enough for a Sicilian. *A.* what opinion? for I do not recollect it. *M.* I will tell you if I can in Latin, for you know I am no more used to bring in Latin sentences in a Greek discourse, than Greek in a Latin one. *A.* And that is right enough: but what is that opinion of Epicharmus?

M. I would not die, but yet
Am not concerned that I shall be dead.

A. I now recollect the Greek, but since you have obliged me to grant that the dead are not miserable, proceed to convince me that it is not miserable to be under a necessity of dying. *M.* That is easy enough, but I have greater things in hand. *A.* How comes that to be so easy? and what are those things of more consequence? *M.* Thus: because, if there is no evil after death, death itself can be none; for what succeeds that immediately, is a state where you grant there is no evil; so that to be obliged to die can be no evil; for that is to arrive there where we allow no evil is. *A.* I beg you will be more explicit on this, for these subtle arguments force me sooner to a concession than conviction; but what are those more important things you undertake? *M.* To teach you, if I can, that death is not only no evil, but a good. *A.* I do not insist on that, but should be glad to hear, for should you not prove your point, yet you may prove that death is no evil: but I will not interrupt you, I should like to hear a continued discourse. *M.* What, if I should ask you a question, would you not answer? *A.* That would have pride in it; but I would rather you should not ask but where necessity requires.

IX. *M.* I will comply with you, and explain as well as I can, what you require; but not like the Pythian Apollo, that what I say must be infallible; but as a mere man, endeavouring at probabilities, by conjecture, for I have no ground to proceed further on, than probability. Let them deal in demonstrations, who say, they can perceive things as they are, and who proclaim themselves philosophers, by profession. *A.* Do as you please, we are ready to hear you. *M.* The first thing is to inquire, what death, which seems to be so well known, is; for some imagine death to be the separation of the soul from the body; some that there is no such separation, but that soul and body perish together, and that the soul is extinguished with the body. Of those who admit of the soul's separation, some are for its immediate departure, some that it continues a time, others for ever: there is great dispute even what the soul is, where it is, and whence it is derived: with some, the heart itself seems to be the soul, hence the expressions, out of heart, bad-hearted, and of one heart; and that prudent Nasica, twice consul, was called Corculus, i. e. wise heart; and Ælius Sextus, a man of noble heart. Empedocles imagines the heart's blood to be the soul; with others, a certain part of the brain seems to be the throne of the soul; others neither allow the heart nor a certain part of the brain to be the soul; but some would have the heart to be the seat and mansion of the soul; others, the brain. Some would have the soul, or spirit, to be air, as we generally do; the name signifying as much, for we say to breathe, to expire, to be animated, &c. and the Latin word for the spirit implies breath.

The soul seems to Zeno, the Stoic, to be fire. But what I have said of the heart's blood, air, and fire, are general opinions: the rest almost singular, of which there were formerly many amongst the ancients.

X. The latest is Aristoxenus, both musician and philosopher; he maintains a certain intension of the body, like what is called harmony in music, to be the soul. Thus, from the figure and nature of the body, various motions are excited, as sounds from an instrument. He stuck close to his profession, and yet he said something, whatever it was, which had been said and explained a great while before by Plato. Xenocrates denied that the soul had any figure, or any thing like matter; but said it was a number, the power of which, as Pythagoras thought, some ages before, was the greatest in nature: his master, Plato, had imagined a three-fold soul; the chief, i. e. reason, he had lodged in the head, as in a tower; and being willing to separate the other two, he placed anger in the breast, and desire under the præcordia. But Dicæarchus, in a discourse of some learned disputants, held at Corinth, which he gives us in three books; in the first of which he makes many speakers; in the other two he introduces a certain Pherecrates, an old man of Phthios, who, as he said, was descended from Deucalion; asserting, that there is in fact no soul; and that it is a name, without a meaning; and that it is idle to say, animals, or animated; that neither men nor beasts have minds or souls; and all that power, by which we act or perceive, is equally infused into every living creature, and is inseparable from the body, for it then would be nothing; nor is there any thing besides one simple body, so fashioned, as to live and have its sensation, from the temperature of nature. Aristotle, superior to all, both in parts and industry, (I always except Plato,) having embraced these four known sorts of principles, from which all things deduce their original, imagines there is a certain fifth nature, from whence comes the soul; for to think, to foresee, to learn, to teach, to invent any thing, and many others; as, to remember, to love, to hate, desire, to fear, to be pleased or displeased; these, and such like, are, he thinks, in none of those four kinds: he adds a fifth kind, which has no name, and thus by a new name he calls the soul ἐντελέχεια, as it were a certain continued and perpetual motion.

XI. If I have not forgotten, these are all the opinions concerning the soul. I have omitted Democritus, a very great man indeed, but who deduces the soul from the fortuitous concourse of light and round corpuscles, as with them, the crowd of atoms can effect every thing. Which of these opinions is true, some god must determine: the great question with us is, which has the most appearance of truth: shall we determine between them; or return to our subject? *A.* I could wish both, if possible; but it is difficult to mix them; therefore, if without a discussion of them we can get rid of the fears of death, let us proceed to do so; but if this is not to be done without explaining the question about souls, let us have that now, the other another time. *M.* I take that to be best, which I perceive you are inclined to; for reason will evince, that let either of the opinions I have stated be true, death cannot be an evil: for, if either the heart, the blood, or brain, be the soul, certainly, as corporeal, it will perish with the rest of the body; if it should be air, it will be dispersed; if fire, extinguished; if Aristoxenus's harmony, disconcerted. What shall I say of Dicæarchus, who denies there is any soul? In all these opinions, there is nothing to affect any one after death; for all feeling is lost with life, and where there is no sensation, nothing can interfere to affect us. The opinions of others are charged with hope; if it is any pleasure to you to think, that souls, after they leave the body, may go to heaven as their abode. *A.* I have great pleasure in that thought, and it is what I most desire; but should it not be so, I still am very willing to believe it. *M.* What occasion have you then for my assistance? am I superior to Plato in eloquence? Turn over carefully his book that treats of the soul, you will have there all you can want. *A.* I have indeed done that, and often; but I know not how, I allow of it whilst I am reading; but when I lay down the book, and begin to reflect with myself on the immortality of the soul, that conviction vanishes. *M.* How comes that? do you admit that souls exist after death, or that they perish in death? *A.* I agree to that. *M.* What if they should exist? *A.* I allow them happy. *M.* If they perish? *A.* I cannot think they are unhappy, because they have no existence. You drove me to that concession but just now. *M.* How then can you maintain any suspicions of death being a misery, which either makes us happy, the soul continuing; or not unhappy, as void of all sensation?

XII. *A.* Explain therefore, if it is not troublesome, first, if you can, that souls exist; then, should you fail in that, for it is very difficult, that death is free of all evil; for I am not without my fears, that this itself is an evil; I do not say, the immediate deprivation of sense, but, that we shall be deprived. *M.* I have the best authority in support of the opinion you desire to have established, which ought, and generally has, great weight in all cases. And first, I have all antiquity on that side; which the nearer it is to its origin and divine descent, possibly by that discerns truth the clearer: this very thing, then, was adopted by all those ancients, whom Ennius calls, in the Sabine tongue, Casci; that in death there was a sensation, and that, when men departed this life, they were not so entirely destroyed, as to perish absolutely. And this may appear, as from many other things, so from the pontifical rites, and funeral obsequies, which men of the best sense would not have been so solicitous about, nor fenced from any injury with such severe laws, but from a firm persuasion, that death was not so entire a destruction as to leave nothing remaining, but a certain transmigration, as it were, and change of life; which usually conveyed the illustrious of both sexes into heaven, confining others to the earth, but so as still to exist. From this, and the sentiments of the Romans,

In heaven Romulus with gods now lives,

Ennius saith, on common report: hence Hercules is held so great and propitious a god amongst the Greeks, from whom we received him, as he is also by those who inhabit the borders of the ocean. Hence Bacchus was deified, the offspring of Semele; and from the same illustrious fame we receive Castor and Pollux, as gods, who are reported not only to have helped the Romans to victory in their battles, but to have been the messengers of their success. What? Ino, the daughter of Cadmus, is she not called Leucothea, by the Greeks, and Matuta, by us? What? is not all heaven (not to dwell on particulars) filled, as it were, with the offspring of men?

XIII. Should I attempt to search into antiquity, and produce from thence, what the Greek writers have asserted; it would appear that even those who are called their principal gods, went from hence into heaven: examine the sepulchres of them which are shewn in

Greece; recollect, as you are initiated, what is delivered in the mysteries; then will you perceive how extensive this doctrine is. But they who were not acquainted with physics, (for they began to be in vogue many ages after,) had no higher conviction than what natural reason could give them; they were not in possession of the reason and cause of things; they were often induced by certain visions, and those generally in the night, to think that they were still alive, who had departed from this life. And this may further be brought as an irrefragable argument, that there are gods, in that there never was any nation so barbarous, not a single instance of that savageness, as to be without some notion of gods: many have wrong notions of the gods, which may proceed from bad customs, yet all allow there is a certain divine nature and energy; nor doth this proceed from conversing together, or consent of parties; it is not an opinion established by law: and in every case the consent of all nations is to be looked on as a law of nature. Who is there then that does not lament the loss of his friends, principally from imagining them deprived of the conveniences of life? Take away this opinion, and you remove with it all grief; for no one grieves on his own account. Perhaps we may be slightly affected, and uneasy; but that bitter lamentation, and those bewailing tears, have their cause from our apprehensions, that he, whom we loved, is deprived of the advantages of life, and is sensible of it. And we are led to this opinion by nature, without learning, or the deductions of reason.

XIV. But the greatest argument is, that nature herself gives a silent judgment in favour of the immortality of the soul, in that all are anxious, and greatly so, in what relates to futurity:

One plants, what future ages shall enjoy,

as Statius saith, in his Synephebi. What has he an eye to in this, but that he is interested in posterity? Shall the industrious husbandman then plant trees, the fruit of which he shall never see? and shall not the great man found laws, institutes, a republic? What doth the procreation of children imply? the continuing a name—adoptions—the exactness in writing wills? what the inscriptions on monuments, or elogies? but that our thoughts run on futurity? There is no doubt but a judgment may be formed of nature in general, from those of the best natural dispositions; and what is a better natural disposition in man, than those discover, who look on themselves born for the protection, preservation, and assistance of others? Hercules went to heaven; he never had gone thither, had he not, whilst amongst men, secured that road to himself.—These are of old date, and have, besides, the sanction of religion.

XV. What, do you imagine so many and such great men of our republic, who have sacrificed their lives for its good, thought that their names should not continue beyond their lives? None ever encountered death for their country, but under a firm persuasion of immortality! Themistocles might have lived at his ease; so might Epaminondas; and, not to look abroad for instances and amongst the ancients, I myself might. But, I know not how, there adheres to our minds a certain presage of future ages; and this both exists most, and appears clearest, in men of the best parts, and greatest souls. Take away this, and who is so mad as to spend his life amidst toils and dangers? I speak of those in power. What were the poet's views but to be ennobled after death? Whence then have we,

> Behold old Ennius here, who erst
> Thy fathers' great exploits rehears'd.

He challenged the reward of glory from those whose ancestors he had ennobled. And thus the same poet,

> Let none with tears my funeral grace, for I
> Claim from my works an immortality.

Why do I mention poets? the very mechanics are desirous of fame after death: why did Phidias include a model of himself, in the shield of Minerva, when he was not allowed to inscribe his name on it? What did our philosophers mean, when they put their names to those very books they wrote on the contempt of glory? If, then, universal consent is the voice of nature, and it is the general opinion every where, that those who have quitted this life, are still interested in something; we must subscribe to that opinion. And if we think men of the greatest abilities and virtue see clearest into nature, as her most perfect work; it is very probable, as every great man endeavours most for the public good, that there is something he will be sensible of after death.

XVI. But as we naturally think there are gods, and what they are, we discover by reason; so, by the consent of nations, we are induced to believe, that our souls survive; but where their habitation is, and what they are, must be learned from reason; the want of which knowledge has given rise to the infernals, and birth to those fears which you seem, not without reason, to despise: for our bodies falling to the ground, and being covered with earth, from whence they are said to be interred, have occasioned them to imagine that the dead continue, the remainder of their existence, under ground; which opinion of theirs has drawn after it many errors; which the poets have increased; for the theatre, crowded with women and children, has been greatly affected on hearing these pompous verses,

> Lo! here I am, who scarce could gain this place,
> Thro' stony mountains, and a dreary waste;
> Thro' clifts, whose sharpen'd stones tremendous hung,
> Where dreadful darkness spread itself around:

and the error prevailed so much, which indeed at present seems to me to be removed, that although they knew the bodies were burned, yet they conceived such things to be done in the infernal regions, as could not be executed or imagined without a body; for they could not apprehend, how unbodied souls could exist; and therefore, they looked out for some shape or figure. From hence all that account of the dead in Homer; hence my friend Appius framed his Necromancy; hence the lake of Avernus, in my neighbourhood;

> From whence the souls of undistinguished shape,
> No mortal blood, rush from the open gate
> Of Acheron, and to this world escape.

And they must needs have these appearances speak, which is not possible, without a tongue, a palate, jaws, without the help of lungs and sides, or without some shape or figure; for they could see nothing by their mind alone, they referred all to their eyes. To withdraw the mind from sensual objects, and abstract our thoughts from what we are accustomed to, is the property of a great genius: I am persuaded there were many such in former ages: but Pherecydes, the Syrian, is the first on record, who said that the souls of men were immortal; he was of great antiquity, in the reign of my namesake Tullus. His disciple, Pythagoras, greatly confirmed this opinion, who came into Italy, in the reign of Tarquin the Proud; and all that country which is called Great Greece, was held by him in honour and discipline, and under great submission to his authority: and the Pythagorean sect was many ages after in so great credit, that all learning was confined to that name.

XVII. But I return to the ancients: They scarce ever gave any reason for their opinion, but what could be explained by numbers and characters. It is reported of Plato, that he came into Italy, to acquaint himself with the Pythagoreans; and that when there, amongst others, he made an acquaintance with Archytas and Timæus, and learned from them all the tenets of the Pythagoreans: that he not only was of the same opinion with Pythagoras, concerning the immortality of the soul, but he brought reasons in support of it; which, if you have nothing to say against it, I will pass over, and drop all this hope of immortality. *A.* What, will you leave me, when you have raised my expectations so high? I had rather, so help me Hercules, be mistaken with Plato, whom I know how much you esteem, and whom I admire, from what you say of him, than be in the right with them. *M.* I commend you: for indeed, I could myself willingly be mistaken with him. Do we then doubt of this as of other things? though I think here is very little room for doubt; for the mathematicians assure us, that the earth is placed in the midst of the world, as it were a point, which they call a *κεντρον*, surrounded by the whole heavens: and that such is the nature of the four principles of all things, that they have equally divided amongst them, the constituents of all bodies. That earthly and humid bodies are carried at equal angles, by their own propensity and weight, into the earth and sea; the other two parts are of fire and air. As the two former are carried by their gravity and weight, into the middle region of the world; so these, on the other hand, ascend by right lines, into the celestial regions; either naturally endeavouring at the highest place, or that lighter bodies are naturally repelled by heavier, which being the case, it must evidently be, that souls, admitting them to be animals, i. e. to breathe, or of the nature of fire, must mount upwards: but should the soul be a number, which it is said to be, with more subtlety than clearness; or that fifth nature, rather without a name than not understood; still it is too pure and perfect, not to arrive at a great distance from the earth. Something of this sort, then, the soul is, that so active a principle should not lie immerged in the heart or brain; or, as Empedocles would have it, in the blood.

XVIII. We will pass over Dicæarchus, with his contemporary and fellow-disciple Aristoxenus, both indeed men of learning. One of them seems never to have been affected with grief, as he could not perceive that he had a soul; the other is so pleased with his musical compositions, that he endeavours to shew an analogy betwixt them and souls. We may understand harmony to arise from the intervals of sounds, whose various compositions occasion many harmonies; but I do not see how a disposition of members, and the figure of a body without a soul, can occasion harmony; he had better, learned as he is, leave this to his master Aristotle, and follow his trade, as a musician; good advice is given him in that Greek proverb,

Apply your talents where you best are skilled.

I will have nothing at all to do with that fortuitous concourse of individual light, and round corpuscles, notwithstanding Democritus insists on their being warm, and having breath, i. e. life. But this soul, should it consist of either of the four principles, from which we deduce all things, is of inflamed air, as seems particularly to have been the opinion of Panætius, and must necessarily mount upwards, for air and fire have no tendency downwards, and always ascend: so should they be dissipated, that must be at some distance from the earth; but should they remain, and preserve their state, it is clearer still that they must be carried heavenward; and this gross and concrete air, which is nearest the earth, must be divided and broke by them; for the soul is warmer, or rather hotter than that air, which I just now called gross and concrete; which is evident from this, that our bodies, compounded of the terrene kind of principles, grow warm by the heat of the soul.

XIX. I add, that the soul may the easier escape from this air, which I have often named, and break through it; because nothing is swifter than the soul; no swiftness is comparable to that of the soul; which, should it remain uncorrupt, and without alteration, must necessarily be carried with that velocity, as to penetrate and divide all this region, where clouds, and rain, and winds are formed; which by means of exhalations from the earth, is moist and dark: which region, when the soul has once got above, and falls in with, and perceives a nature like its own, being compounded of thin air, and a moderate solar heat, it rests with these fires, and endeavours no higher flight. For when it has attained a lightness and heat like its own, it moves no more, balanced as it were between two equal weights. That then is its natural seat where it has penetrated to something like itself; where, wanting nothing else, it may be supported and maintained by the aliments, which nourish and maintain the stars. As we are used to be incited to all sorts of desires, by the stimulus of the body, and the more so, as we envy those who are in possession of what we long for, we shall certainly be happy, when with this body we get rid of these desires and provocatives; which is our case at present, when, dismissing all other cares, we curiously examine and look into any thing; which we shall then do with greater ease; and employ ourselves entirely in viewing and considering things; because there is naturally in our minds a certain insatiable desire of seeing truth; and the very region itself, where we shall arrive, as it gives us a more intuitive view of celestial things, will raise our desires after knowledge. For this beauty of the heavens, even here on earth, gave birth to that philosophy, which Theophrastus calls an inheritance, both from father and mother; greatly raised by a desire of knowledge. But they will in a particular manner enjoy this, who, whilst inhabitants of this world, enveloped in darkness, were desirous of looking into these things with the eye of their mind.

XX. For if they now think they have attained something, who have seen the mouth of the Pontus, and those straits which were passed by the ship called Argo, because,

> From Argos she did chosen men convey,
> Bound to fetch back the golden fleece their prey.

Or they, who saw the straits of the ocean,

> Where the swift waves divide the neighbouring shores
> Of Europe and of Afric.——

What kind of sight, then, do you imagine that to be, when the whole earth is viewed? not only in its position, form, and boundaries; those parts of it that are habitable, but those also that lie cultivated, through the extremities of heat and cold: for what we now see we do not view with our eyes; for body itself has no sensation: but as the naturalists, nay, even the physicians assure us, who have opened our bodies, and examined them, there are certain perforated canals, from the seat of the soul to the eyes, ears, and nose; so that frequently, when either prevented by meditation, or the force of some bodily disorder, we neither hear nor see, though our eyes and ears are open, and in good condition; so that we may easily apprehend that it is the soul that sees and hears; not those parts, which are but windows to the soul; by means of which the soul can perceive nothing, unless she is on the spot, and exerts herself. How shall we account, that by the same power of thinking, we comprehend the most difficult things; as colour, taste, heat, smell, and sound? which the soul could never know by her five messengers, unless every thing was referred to it, and she was sole judge of all. And we shall certainly discover these things, clearer, and more perfect, when the soul, disengaged from the body, shall arrive there, where nature leads; for at present, notwithstanding nature has contrived, with the greatest skill, those canals which lead from the body to the soul; yet are they, in some way or other, stopped up with concrete and terrene bodies: but when we shall be nothing but soul, nothing will interfere, to prevent our seeing every thing as it is.

XXI. It is true, I might expatiate, did the subject require it, on the many and various objects the soul will be entertained with in those heavenly regions; when I reflect on which, I am apt to wonder at the boldness of some philosophers, who are so struck with the knowledge of nature, as to thank, in an exulting manner, the first inventor of natural philosophy, and reverence him as a god: for they declare themselves freed, by his means, from the greatest tyrants, a perpetual terror, and a fear that molested them, by night and day. What is this dread? this fear? what old woman is there so weak as to fear these things, which you, forsooth, had you not been acquainted with physics, would stand in awe of?

The hallow'd roofs of Acheron, the dread
Of Orcus, and the pale sejour of the dead.

And doth it become a philosopher to boast that he is not afraid of these, and has discovered them to be false? Hence we may know how acute they were by nature, who, without learning, had attained to these things. They have gained, I know not what, who have learned, that when they die, they shall perish entirely; which being admitted, for I say nothing to it, what is there agreeable or glorious in it? Not that I see any reason why Pythagoras and Plato's opinion might not be true: but should Plato have assigned no reason, (observe how much I esteem the man,) the weight of his authority would have borne me down; but he has brought so many reasons, that, to me, he appears to have endeavoured to convince others; himself he certainly did.

XXII. But there are many who labour the other side of the question, and condemn souls to death, as capitally convicted; nor have they any better argument, against the eternity of the soul, than their not being able to conceive a soul without a body; as if they could really conceive, what it is in the body; its form, size, and seat: that were they able to have a full view of all that is now hid from them in a living body, the soul would be discernible by them; or, is it of so fine a contexture as to evade their sight? Let those consider this, who deny they can form any idea of the soul, without the body, if they can conceive what it is in the body. As to my own part, when I reflect on the nature of the soul, I am more distressed to conceive what it is in the body, a place that doth not belong to it, than what it is when it leaves it, and is arrived at the free æther, its own habitation, as it were. Could we apprehend nothing but what we see, certainly we could form no notion of God, nor of the divine soul, freed from body. Dicæarchus indeed, and Aristoxenus, because it was hard to understand the soul, and its properties, asserted there was no soul. It is indeed the most difficult thing imaginable, to discern the soul, by the soul. And this, doubtless, is the meaning of the precept of Apollo, which advises every one to know himself. I do not apprehend his intention to have been, that we should inform ourselves of our members, our stature, and make; nor doth self imply our bodies; nor do I, who speak thus to you, address myself to your body: when, therefore, he saith, "Know yourself," he saith this, inform yourself of the nature of your soul; for the body is but a kind of vessel, or receptacle of the soul: whatever your soul doth, is your own act. To know the soul, then, unless it had been divine, would not have been a precept of that excellent wisdom, as to be attributed to a god; but should the soul not know what itself is, will you say that it doth not perceive itself to be? that it has motion? on which is founded that reason of Plato's, which is explained by Socrates, in Phædrus, and inserted by me, in my sixth book of the Republic.

XXIII. That which is always moved, is eternal; but that which gives motion to another, and is moved itself from some other cause, when that motion ceases, must necessarily cease to exist. That, then alone, which is self-moved, because it is never forsaken by itself, must continue to be always moved. Besides, it is the fountain and beginning of motion to every thing else: but whatever is first, has no beginning, for all things arise from that first; itself cannot owe its rise to any thing else; for it would not be the first, had it proceeded from any thing else. If it had no beginning, it never will have end; for the original being extinguished, itself cannot be restored from any thing else, nor produce any thing from itself; inasmuch as all things must necessarily arise from that first cause. Thus it comes about, that the beginning of motion must arise from itself, because it is itself, moved by itself; and that can neither have a beginning, nor cease to be; otherwise the whole heavens would be overset, and all nature stand still, nor be able to acquire any force, by the impulse of which it might be first set in motion. Seeing then it is clear, that whatever moves itself, is eternal; can there be any doubt that the soul is so? for that is inanimate, which is moved by an external force; but every animal is moved by an interior force, and its own. For this is the peculiar nature and power of the soul; which, if it be the property of the soul alone to have self-motion, certainly it never had a beginning, and is eternal. Should all the lower order of philosophers, for so I think they may be called, who dissent from Plato and Socrates, and that school, unite their force; they never would be able to explain any thing so elegantly, nor even understand how artfully this conclusion is drawn. The soul then perceives itself to have motion, and with that perception is sensible that it is moved, by its own, and not the agency of another; and it is impossible that it should ever forsake itself; from whence arises eternity, unless you have something to say against it. *A.* I should myself be very well pleased, not to have a thought arise in my mind against it, I am so much inclined to that opinion.

XXIV. *M.* I appeal to you, if these arguments that prove there is something divine in the soul, are not as strong? which divine properties, could I account how they begun, I might also how they might cease to be; for I think I can account how the blood, bile, phlegm, bones, nerves, veins, all the limbs, and shape of the whole body, were concreted and made; nay, the soul itself, were there nothing more in it than a principle of life, might be put upon the same footing as a vine or tree, and accounted for as naturally; for these, as we say, live. Besides, were desires and aversions all that belonged to the soul, they are but in common with the beasts; but it has, in the first place, memory, and that so infinite, as to retain numberless things, which Plato would have to be a recollection of a former life; for in that book which is inscribed Menon, Socrates asks a child some questions in geometry, of measuring a square; his answers are such as a child would make, and yet his questions are so easy, that, answering them, one by one, he is as ready, as if he had learned geometry. From whence Socrates would infer, that learning implies only recollection, which he explains more accurately, in the discourse he held the very day he died; for any one entirely illiterate, to answer a question well, that is proposed to him, manifestly shews that he doth not learn it then, but recollects it by his memory. Nor is it accountable any other way, how children come to have notions of so many and such important things, as are implanted, or as it were sealed up in their minds; which the Greeks call common notions, unless the soul before it entered the body had been well stored with knowledge; for he holds that not to be, which has a beginning and ending; and that alone to be, which is always the same; and what he calls an idea, we a quality. The soul, then, shut up in the body, could not discover, but brought with it, what it knows: so that we are no longer surprised at its extensive knowledge; nor doth the soul clearly discover its ideas at its first resort to this troublesome and unusual dwelling; but after having refreshed and recollected itself, it then by its memory recovers them; therefore to learn, implies only to recollect. But I am in a particular manner surprised at memory; for what is that by which we remember? what is its force? what its nature? I am not inquiring, how great a memory Simonides may be said to have had; how great Theodectes; how great that Cineas, who came ambassador here from Pyrrhus; or lately, Charmadas; or very lately, Sceptius Metrodorus; how great our Hortensius: I speak of common memory, and principally of those, who are employed in any considerable study or art, of the capacity of whose minds it is hard to judge, they remembered so many things.

XXV. Should you ask what this leads to? I think we may understand what that power is, (for Plato constantly maintains the body to be nothing,) and whence we have it. It certainly proceeds neither from the heart, nor blood, nor brain, nor atoms; whether it be air or fire, I know not; nor am I, like those, ashamed to own where I am ignorant, that I am so. Were it possible to determine in any doubtful affair, I would swear that the soul, be it air or fire, is divine. What? I beseech you, can you imagine so great a power of memory to be sown in, or be of the composition of earth? or this dark and gloomy atmosphere? Though you cannot apprehend what it is, yet you see what kind of thing it is, or if not that, yet you certainly see how great it is. What then? shall we imagine, there is a kind of measure in the soul, into which, as into a vessel, all we remember is poured? that indeed is absurd. How shall we form any idea of the bottom, or any of such a shape or fashion of the soul? or how any at all of its holding so much? Shall we imagine the soul to receive impressions like wax, and memory to be marks of the impressions made on the soul? What are the characters of words, what of things themselves? or where is that prodigious immensity as to give impressions to so many things? What, lastly, is that power which discovers, and is called invention? Doth he seem to be compounded of this earthly, mortal, and perishing nature, who first invented names for every thing, which with Pythagoras is the highest pitch of wisdom? or he, who collected the dispersed inhabitants of the world, and called them together into social life? or he, who confined the sounds of the voice, which are infinite, to the marks of a few letters? or who observed the courses of the planets, their progressive motions, their laws? These were all great men; but they were greater still, who invented food, raiment, houses; who introduced civility amongst us, and armed us against the wild beasts; by whom being civilized and polished, we proceeded from the necessaries of life to its embellishments. For we have provided great entertainments for the ears, by inventing and qualifying the variety and nature of sounds. We view the stars, as well those that are fixed, as those which are called improperly wandering. The soul that is acquainted with their revolutions and motions, acquaints itself that it is like his, who devised those stars in the heavens: for when Archimedes described in a sphere the motions of the moon, sun, and five planets, he did the same as Plato's god, in his Timæus, who made the world; he adjusted motions of different slowness, and velocities, in one circle. Now allowing that what we see in the world, could not be effected without a god, Archimedes could not have imitated the same motions, in his sphere, without a divine soul.

XXVI. To me, indeed, it appears, that those studies

which are more known, and in greater esteem, are not without some divine energy: so that I scarce think a poet who produces an approved poem, to be without some divine impulse on his mind; or that oratory, abounding with sonorous words, and fruitful sentences, could flow thus, without some greater force. What then is philosophy? which is the parent of all arts, but as Plato saith, a gift, as I express it, an invention of the gods? This taught us, first, the worship of them; then justice, which arises from men's being formed into society; next modesty, and elevation of soul. Philosophy dispersed darkness from our souls, as it were from our eyes, enabling us to see all things that are above or below; the beginning, end, and middle of every thing. I am convinced entirely, that what could effect so many, and such great things, must be divine. For what is a memory of words and things? what also invention? even that than which nothing greater can be conceived in a god! for I do not imagine the gods to be delighted with nectar and ambrosia, or with Juventas presenting them with a cup; nor do I pay any attention to Homer, who said that Ganymede was carried away by the gods, on account of his beauty, to give Jove his drink. Too weak reasons for doing Laomedon such injury! These were mere inventions of Homer, who gave his gods the imperfections of men. I wish he had given men the perfections of the gods! those perfections I mean of uninterrupted health, wisdom, invention, memory. Therefore the soul is, as I say, divine; or as Euripides more boldly expresses it, a god. And thus, if the divinity be air or fire, the soul of man is the same: for as that celestial nature has nothing earthly or humid, so the soul of man is also void of all these: but if it is of that certain fifth nature, first introduced by Aristotle, both gods and souls are of the same.

XXVII. As this is my opinion, I have explained it in these very words, in my book of Consolation. The origin of the soul of man is not to be found in any thing earthy, for there is nothing in the soul mixt or concrete, or that has any appearance of being formed or made out of the earth; nothing even humid, airy, fiery; for what is there in such like natures, that has the power of memory, understanding, or thought? that can recollect the past; foresee future things; and comprehend the present? which are divine properties alone; nor can we discover whence men could have these, but from God. There is therefore a peculiar nature and power in the soul, distinct from those natures, more known and familiar to us. Whatever then that is, which thinks, which has understanding, volition, and a principle of life, is heavenly and divine, and on that account must necessarily be eternal: nor can God himself, who is known to us, be conceived otherwise, than a soul free and unembarrassed, distinct from all mortal concretion, acquainted with every thing, and giving motion to it, itself endued with perpetual motion.

XXVIII. Of this kind and nature is the soul of man. Should you be asked then, what this soul is? where is your own? or what is it? what answer can I make? If I have not faculties for knowing all that I could desire to know, you will allow me, I hope, to make use of those I have. The soul is not equal to the discerning of itself; yet the soul, like the eye, though it has no reflex view of itself, sees other things: it doth not see (which is of least consequence) its own shape; perhaps not; though it possibly may; but we will pass that by: but it certainly sees that it has vigour, sagacity, memory, motion, velocity; these are all great, divine, eternal properties. What its appearance is, or where it dwells, is not matter of inquiry. As when we behold, first the lucid appearance of the heavens; then, the vast velocity of its revolutions, beyond the imagination of our thought; the vicissitudes of nights and days; the four-fold division of the seasons, adapted to the ripening of the fruits of the earth, and the temperature of our bodies: and then look up to the sun, the moderator and governor of all these; view the moon, by the increase and decrease of its light, marking as it were, and appointing our holy days; and see the five planets, carried in the same circle, divided into twelve parts, preserving invariably the same courses, with dissimilar motions amongst themselves; and the nightly appearance of the heaven, adorned on all sides with stars; then, the globe of the earth, raised above the sea, placed in the centre of the universe, inhabited and cultivated in its two opposite extremities; one of them, the place of our habitation, situated to the north pole, under the seven stars:

> Where the cold northern blasts, with horrid sound,
> Harden to ice the snowy covered ground.

The other, the south pole, unknown to us, called by the Greeks *αντιχθονα:* other parts, uncultivated, because either frozen with cold, or burnt up with heat; but where we dwell, it never fails in its season,

> To yield a placid sky, to bid the trees
> Assume the lively verdure of their leaves:
> The vine to bud, and, joyful in its shoots,
> Foretell the approaching vintage of its fruits:
> The ripened corn to sing, whilst all around
> Full riv'lets glide; and flowers deck the ground.

Then the multitude of cattle, part for food, part for tilling the ground, others for carriage, for clothing; and man himself made as it were on purpose to contemplate the heavens and the gods, and to pay adoration to them; lastly, the whole earth, and wide extending seas, given to man's use.

XXIX. When we view these, and numberless other things, can we doubt that something presides over these, or made them? if they are made, as is the opinion of Plato; or if, as Aristotle thinks, they are eternal; so great a work, and so great a blessing, cannot be supposed, without a director. Thus, though you see not the soul of man, as you see not the Deity; yet as you acknowledge a God, from his works, so own the divine power of the soul, from its remembering things, its invention, the quickness of its motion, and from every charm of virtue. But where is it seated? say you. In my opinion it is in the head, and I can bring you reasons for that opinion; but of those elsewhere. At present, let the soul reside where it will, you certainly have one in you. Should you ask what its nature is? It has one peculiarly its own; but admitting it to be of fire, or air, it doth not affect the question; only observe this, as you are convinced there is a God, though you are ignorant where he resides, and what shape he is of; so you should be assured you have a soul, though you cannot satisfy yourself of the place of its residence, nor the fashion of it. In our knowledge of the soul, unless we are grossly ignorant in physics, we cannot but be satisfied that it has nothing but what is simple, unmixed, uncompounded; which being admitted, it cannot be separated, nor divided, dispersed or parted, and therefore cannot perish; for to perish implies parting asunder, a division, a disunion of those parts which, whilst it subsisted, were held together by some band. Induced by these and such like reasons, Socrates neither looked out for any body to plead for him, when accused, nor begged any favour from his judges, but maintained a manly freedom, not the effect of pride, but of the true greatness of his soul; and on the last day of his life, he held much discourse on this subject; and a few days before he refused his liberty, when he might have been easily freed from his confinement, and when he had hold, in a manner, of that deadly cup, he spoke, with an air of one not forced to die, but as ascending into heaven.

XXX. For so he thought himself to be, and thus he harangued: "That there are two ways, and that the souls of men, at their departure from the body, took different roads; for those that were polluted with vices, that are common to men, and had given themselves up entirely to unclean desires, blinded by which, they had habituated themselves to all manner of debaucheries, or had laid detestable schemes for the ruin of their country, took a road wide of that which led to the assembly of the gods: but they who had preserved themselves perfect and chaste, and free from the slightest contagion with the body, and had kept themselves always at a distance from it; and whilst on earth, had conformed to the life of the gods; found the return easy to those, from whom they came." Therefore he relates, that all good and wise men should take example from the swans, who are, not without reason, sacred to Apollo; but particularly, because they seem to have received the gift of divination from him, by which, foreseeing how happy it is to die, they leave this world with singing and joy. Nor can any one doubt of this, unless it happens to us who think intensely of the soul, as is common to those who look earnestly at the setting sun, to lose the sight of it entirely: so the mind's eye viewing itself, sometimes grows dull, and for that reason we become remiss in our contemplation. Thus our reasoning is carried like one sailing on the immense ocean, harassed with doubts and anxieties, not knowing how to proceed, but measuring back again those dangerous tracts he had passed. But these reflections are of long standing, and borrowed from the Greeks. Even Cato left this world, as pleased with an opportunity of dying; for that God who presides in us, forbids our departure hence without his leave. But when God himself shall give a just cause, as formerly to Socrates, lately to Cato, and often to many others; certainly every man of sense would gladly exchange this darkness, for that light; not that he would forcibly break from the chains that held him, for that would be against law; but walk out, like one discharged by a magistrate, or some lawful authority. The whole life of a philosopher is, as the same saith, a meditation on death.

XXXI. For what do we else, when we call off our minds from pleasure, i. e. from our attention to the body, from the managing our estates, which we do merely on the body's account; when from duties of a public nature, or from all other employs whatsoever, what, I say, do we else, but invite the soul to reflect on itself? oblige it to converse with itself, and break off its acquaintance with the body? to separate the soul from the body, then, what is it but to learn to die? Wherefore, let me persuade you, to meditate on this, and break off your connexion with the body, i. e. learn to die. This is to be in heaven whilst on earth; and when we shall be carried thither freed from these chains, our souls will make their way with more ease: for they who are always linked thus with the body, even when disengaged make very slow advances, like those who have worn fetters many years; which when we shall arrive at, we shall then live indeed, for this present life is a death, which I could lament, if I might. *A.* You have lamented it sufficiently in your book of Consolation; which, when I read, there is nothing I desire more than to leave these things: but that desire increases, by what I have just now heard. *M.* The time will come, and that soon, whether you hang back or press forward: for time flies. Death is so far from being an evil, as it lately appeared to you, that I suspect, that every thing is a greater evil to man; or nothing a more desirable good; if we become thereby either gods ourselves, or companions of the gods. *A.* This will not do, as there are some who will not allow of it. *M.* But I will not leave off discussing this point, till I have convinced you, that death can upon no account be an evil. *A.* How can it, after what I have known? *M.* Do you ask how it can? there are such swarms of opponents; not only Epicureans, whom I regard very little, but I know not how, almost every man of letters: but my favourite Dicæarchus is very strenuous in opposing the immortality of the soul: for he has written three books, which are entitled Lesbiacs, because the discourse was held at Mitylene, in which he would prove that souls are mortal. Indeed, the Stoics give us as long credit, as the life of a raven; they allow the soul to exist a great while, but are against its eternity.

XXXII. Are you willing to hear, even allowing this, why death cannot be an evil? *A.* As you please; but no one shall force me from my immortality. *M.* I commend you indeed for that; though we should not depend on our opinions: for we are frequently disturbed by some subtle conclusion; we give way and change our opinions in things that are more evident; but in this there is some obscurity. Should any thing of this kind happen, it is well to be on our guard. *A.* You are ght in that, but I will provide against any accident. *M.* Have you any objection to dismissing our friends the Stoics? I mean those, who allow that souls exist after they leave the body, but not always. *A.* Yes, those who admit of the only difficulty in this case, that souls may exist independent of body; but reject that, which is not only very probable, but the consequence of their own concession, that if they may exist some time, they may so for ever. *M.* You take it right; that is the very thing: shall we give therefore any credit to Panætius, when he dissents from his Plato? whom he every where calls divine, the wisest, the most honest of men, the Homer of Philosophers; whom he opposes, in the single opinion of the soul's immortality: For he maintains what nobody denies, that every thing which is generated will perish; that even souls are generated, appears from the resemblance to those that begot them; which is as apparent in the turn of their minds, as their bodies. But he brings another reason; that there is nothing which is sensible of pain, but may also fall ill; but whatever is subject to disorders, is subject to death; the soul is sensible of pain, therefore it may perish.

XXXIII. These may be refuted; for they proceed from his not knowing, that on the subject of the immortality of the soul, he speaks of the mind, which should be free of all turbid motion; not of those parts in which those disorders, anger and lust, have their seat; which he, whom he opposes, imagines to be distinct and separate from the mind. Now this resemblance is more remarkable in beasts, whose souls are void of reason. But the likeness in men consists more in their persons; and it is of no little consequence in what bodies the soul is lodged; for there are many things which depend on the body, that give an edge to the soul, many which blunt it. Aristotle indeed saith, that all men of parts are melancholy; so that I should not have been diplesased to have been somewhat duller than I am. He instances in many, and, as if it were matter of fact, brings his reasons for it: but if the power of those things that proceed from the body, be so great as to influence the mind, (for they are the things, whatever they are, that occasion this likeness,) it doth not necessarily imply, that a similitude of souls should be born. I have done with these likenesses. I wish Panætius could be here; he lived with Africanus; I would inquire of him, which of his family the nephew of Africanus's brother was like? possibly in person like his father; in his manners, so like the most abandoned, that none was more so. Who was the grandson of P. Crassus like, that wise and eloquent man, inferior to none? Or the relations and sons of many other excellent men, whose names there is no occasion to mention? But what are we doing? Have we forgotten, that our purpose was, when we had sufficiently spoke to the immortality of the soul, to evince, that, should the souls perish, there could be, even then, no evil in death? *A.* I remembered it very well; but I had no dislike to your rambling a little from your purpose, whilst you were talking of the soul's immortality.

XXXIV. *M.* I perceive you have sublime thoughts, and would willingly reach heaven; I am not without hopes that such may be our fate. But admit what they assert; that the souls do not remain after death. *A.* Should it be so, I see ourselves deprived of the hopes of a happier life. *M.* But what is there of evil in that opinion? let the soul perish as the body: is there any pain, or indeed any feeling at all in the body after death? no one indeed asserts that; though Epicurus charges Democritus with saying so; but the disciples of Democritus deny it. No sense therefore remains in the soul; for the soul is no where; where then is the evil? for there is nothing but these two. Is it because the separation of the soul and body cannot be effected without pain? but should that be granted, how small is that? yet I think that is false; and that it is very often without any sense, sometimes even with pleasure, and the whole is very trifling, whatever it is, for it is instantaneous. What makes us uneasy, or rather gives us pain, is the leaving all the good things of life. Consider, if I might not more properly say, the evil; what reason is there then to bewail the life of man? and yet I might, with very good reason; but what occasion is there, when I labour to prove that none are miserable after death; to make life more miserable, by lamenting over it? I have done that in the book I wrote, to comfort myself as well as I could. If then our inquiry is after truth, death withdraws us from evil, not from good. This is indeed so copiously handled by Hegesias, the Cyrenian, that he is said to have been forbid by Ptolemy from publishing them in the schools, because some who heard him made away with themselves. There is too an epigram of Callimachus, on Cleombrotus of Ambracia; who, without any misfortune befalling him, as he saith, threw himself from a wall into the sea, on reading a book of Plato's. The book I mentioned of Hegesias, is on men's starving themselves; written on account of somebody who took that method to get rid of life, but, being prevented by his friends, he reckons up to them the miseries of human life: I might do the same, though not so fully as he, who thinks it not worth any man's while to live. I pass over others. Was it even worth my while, for, had I died before I was deprived of the comforts and honours of my own family, and what I received from my public services, death would have taken me from the evils of life, not its blessings?

XXXV. Propose therefore any one, who never knew distress; who never received a blow from fortune: imagine that Metellus, who was honoured with four sons; but Priam had fifty, seventeen of which were legitimate. Fortune had the same power over both, though she exercised it but on one: for Metellus was laid on his funeral pile by many sons and daughters, male and female relations: but Priam fell by the hand of an enemy, after having fled to the altar, deprived of so great a progeny. Had he died before the ruin of his kingdom, his sons alive,

> With all his mighty wealth elate,
> Under rich canopies of state:

would he then have been taken from good or evil? It might seem at that time, from good; yet surely, that would have been to his advantage; nor should we have had these mournful verses,

> Lo! these all perish'd in one flaming pile;
> The foe old Priam did of life beguile,
> And with his blood, thy altar, Jove, defile.

As if any thing better could have happened to him at that time, than to lose his life so; which had it fallen out sooner, would have prevented those consequences; or at least he would have been insensible of them. The case of our friend Pompey was something better; when he fell sick at Naples, the Neapolitans put crowns on their heads, as did those of Puteoli; the people flocked from the country to congratulate him. It is a Grecian custom, and a foolish one; yet it is a sign of good fortune. But the question is, had he died, would he have been taken from good or evil? Certainly from evil. He would not have been engaged in a war with his brother-in-law; he would not have taken up arms before he was prepared; he had not left his own house, nor fled from Italy; he had not, after the loss of his army, fell unarmed into the hands of his enemies, and been put into chains by them: his children had not been destroyed; nor his whole fortune in the possession of the conquerors; who, had he died at that time, had died in all his glory; who, by that delay of death, into what great and terrible misfortunes did he fall?

XXXVI. These things are avoided by death, which though they should never happen, there is a possibility they may; but it never comes into men's heads, that such things may befall them. Every one thinks to be as happy as Metellus; as if the number of the happy exceeded that of the miserable; as if there was any certainty in human affairs; as if there were more rational foundations for hope than fear. But should we grant them even this, that we are by death deprived of good things; must the dead therefore want the good things of life, and be miserable on that account? they must necessarily say so. Can he, who is not, want any thing? To want, has a melancholy sound, and has its force from hence; he had, but has not; he desires, requires, wants. Such are, I suppose, the distresses of one to whom something is wanting, Doth he want eyes? to be blind, is misery. Is he in want of children? not to have them, is misery. This is something with the living, but the dead are neither in want of the blessings of life, nor life itself; I speak of the dead as not existing. But would any say of us, who do exist, that we want horns or wings? Certainly not. Should it be asked, why not? the answer would be, that not to have what neither custom nor nature has fitted you for, would not imply a want of them, though you were sensible you had them not. This argument should be pressed over and over again, that being established, which if souls are mortal, there can be no dispute about; I mean, that the destruction of them by death is so entire, as to remove even the least suspicion of any sense remaining. This then being well grounded and established, we must correctly define what the term, to want, means; that there may be no mistake in the word. To want, then, signifies this; to be without that, you would be glad to have; for inclination for any thing is implied in the word want; excepting when we say in a different sense of the word, that a fever is wanting to any one. For it admits of a different interpretation, when you are without a certain thing, and are sensible you are without it; but yet can easily dispense with your not having it. You cannot apply this expression to the dead, that they want; or that they lament on that account. This is said, that they want a good, which is an evil to them. But a living man doth not want a good, unless he is distressed without it; and yet, we may understand, how any man alive may want a kingdom. When I assert this of you, I cannot use too much art in expressing myself: the case is different with regard to Tarquin, when he was driven from his kingdom: but quite incomprehensible, as to the dead. For to want, implies to be sensible; but the dead are insensible; therefore the dead can be in no want.

XXXVII. But what occasion is there to philosophize here, when philosophy is so little concerned in it? How often have not only our generals, but whole armies, rushed on certain death? which, were it to be feared, L. Brutus had not fell in fight, to prevent the return of that tyrant he had expelled: Decius the father, had not been slain in fighting with the Latins: nor had his son, when engaged with the Etruscans, or his nephew with Pyrrhus, exposed themselves to the enemy's darts. Spain had not seen the Scipios fall in one campaign, fighting for their country; the plains of Cannæ, Paulus and Geminus; Venusia, Marcellus; the Latins, Albinus, nor the Lucani Gracchus. But are any of these miserable now? nay, not even then, after they had breathed their last: nor can any one be miserable after he has lost all sense. But as to that, that it is afflicting to be without sense! it would be so, if the meaning was that any one was really in want of it, but as it is evident there can be nothing in that, which has no existence; what can there be afflicting in that which can neither want, nor be sensible? We should have had this over too often, but that here lies all that the soul shudders at, from the fear of death. For whoever can clearly apprehend, which is as manifest as the light; that when both soul and body are consumed, and there is a total destruction; that which was an animal, becomes nothing; will clearly see, that there is no difference between a Hippocentaur, which never had existence, and king Agamemnon; and that M. Camillus is no more concerned about this present civil war, than I was at the sacking of Rome, when he was in being. Why then should Camillus be affected with the thoughts of these things happening three hundred and fifty years after? And why should I be uneasy at the thoughts of some nation possessing itself of this city, ten thousand years hence? Because so great is our regard for our country, as not to be measured by our own feeling, but by the actual safety of it.

XXXVIII. Death, then, which threatens us daily, from a thousand accidents, and by the very shortness of life cannot be far off, doth not deter a wise man from making provision for his country and his family, that may extend to distant ages, and from regarding posterity, of which he may have no sensation. Wherefore a man may, though persuaded that his soul is mortal, act for eternity, not from a desire of glory, which he will be insensible of, but from a principle of virtue, which glory will attend, though that is not his view. In nature indeed it is thus; as our birth was the beginning of things with us, death will be the end; and as we were no ways concerned with them before we were born, so we shall have none after we are dead: consider thus, where can be the evil? seeing death has no connexion with either the dead, or yet those that are alive: the one are not, the other have nothing to do with it. They who make the least of death, compare it to sleep; as if any one would live ninety years on condition, that at the expiration of sixty, he would sleep out the remainder. The very swine would not accept of life on those terms, much less I: Endymion indeed, if you listen to fables, slept once on a time, on Latmus, a mountain of Caria. I imagine he is not as yet awake. Do you think he is concerned at the moon's being in labour, by whom he was thrown into that sleep, that she might embrace him in that circumstance; for what should he be concerned for who has no sense? You look on sleep as an image of death, and you take that on you daily; and have you any doubt of there being no sense in death, when you see there is none in sleep, which resembles it?

XXXIX. Away then with those follies that speak the old woman; that it is miserable to die before our time. What time do you mean? That of nature? She lent you life, as money, without fixing a time for its payment. Have you any grounds of complaint then, that she recalls it at her pleasure? For you received it on these terms. They that complain thus, allow, that to die in childhood is tolerable; if in the cradle, more so; and yet nature has been more exact with them in demanding back what she gave. They answer by saying, such have not tasted the sweets of life; the other had great expectations from what he had already enjoyed. They judge better in other things, and allow a part to be preferable to none? why not so in life? Though Callimachus is not amiss in saying, more tears had flowed from Priam, than his son; yet they are thought happier who have lived to old age. It would be hard to say why; for I do not apprehend the remainder of life would be happier with any. There is nothing more agreeable to a man than prudence, which old age as certainly strips him of, as any thing else: but what age is long? or what is there at all long to a man? Doth not

> Old age, tho' unregarded, still attend
> On childhood's pastimes, as the cares of men?

But because there is nothing beyond old age, we call that long: all these things are said to be long or short, according to the proportion of time, the time of life they bear, they were given us for. Aristotle saith, there is a kind of insect, near the river Hypanis, which runs from a certain part of Europe into the Pontus, whose life consists but of one day; those that die at the eighth hour, die in full age; those who die when the sun sets, very old, especially when the days are at the longest. Compare our longest age with eternity, and we shall be found as short-lived as those little animals.

XL. Let us then despise all these follies, for what softer name can I give to such levities? and let us lay the foundation of our happiness in the strength and greatness of our minds, in a contempt and disregard for all earthly things, and in the practice of every virtue.

For at present we are enervated by the delicacy of our imaginations, so that, should we leave this world before the promises of our fortune-tellers are made good to us, we should think ourselves deprived of some great advantages, and seem disappointed and forlorn. But if through life we are in continual suspense, still expecting, still desiring, and are in continual pain and torture: good gods! how pleasant must that journey be, which ends in security and ease! How pleased am I with Theramenes! of how exalted a soul he appears! Though we never read of him without tears; yet that excellent man is not to be lamented in his death; who, when imprisoned by the command of the thirty tyrants, drank off at one draught, as if he had been thirsty, the poisoned cup, and threw the remainder out of it, with such force, that it sounded as it fell. On hearing the sound of it, he with a smile said, "I drink this to the handsome Critias;" who had been the most severe against him: for it is customary with the Greeks, at their banquets, to name the person to whom they intend to deliver the cup. This excellent man was pleasant to the last, even when he had received the poison into his bowels; and truly foretold his death, to whom he drank of the poison, which soon followed. Who that thought death an evil, could approve of the evenness of temper in this great man, at the instant of dying! Socrates came a few years after to the same prison and the same cup, by the like iniquity of his judges, as Theramenes by that of the tyrants. What a speech is that which Plato makes him use before his judges, after they had condemned him to death?

XLI. "I am not without hopes, O judges, that it is a favourable circumstance to me, that I am condemned to die: for one of these two things must necessarily be, that either death will deprive me entirely of all sense; or by dying I shall go hence into some other place; wherefore, if I am deprived of sense, and death is like that sleep, which sometimes is so undisturbed, as to be even without the visions of dreams; good gods! what gain is it to die! or what length of days can be preferable to such a night? And if the constant course of future time should resemble that night, who is happier than I am? but if what is said be true, that death is but a removal to those regions where the souls of the departed dwell; that still must be more happy; to have escaped from those who call themselves judges, and to appear before such as are truly so, Minos, Rhadamanthus, Æacus, Triptolemus; and to meet with those who have lived with justice and probity! Can this change of abode appear otherwise than great to you? to converse with Orpheus, Musæus, Homer, Hesiod, is a privilege of inestimable value! I would willingly, were it possible, die often, in order to prove the certainty of what I speak of. What satisfaction must it be to meet with Palamedes, Ajax, and others, betrayed by the iniquity of their judges? I would prove the wisdom even of that king of kings, who led such troops to Troy, that of Ulysses and Sisyphus: nor should I be condemned, as I was here, for such an inquiry. And as for you, my judges, who have absolved me, ye need not fear death, for nothing bad can befall a good man, whether dead or living, nor are his concerns overlooked by the gods, nor has this befallen me by chance; nor have I aught to charge those with, who accused or condemned me, but their intention of doing me harm." In this manner he proceeded; but nothing I more admire than his last words, "But it is time," saith he, "for me, to go hence to death; you, to your employs of life: the immortal gods know which is best; indeed I believe no mortal doth."

XLII. I had preferred this man's soul to all the fortunes of those who sat in judgment on him: notwithstanding he saith the gods only knew which was best, he himself did; for he had determined that before; but he held to the last, the maxim peculiar to him, of affirming nothing. And let us hold to this, not to think any thing an evil, that is a general provision of nature: and let us assure ourselves, that if death is an evil, it is an eternal evil; for death seems to be the end of a miserable life; but if death is a misery, there can be no end. But why do I mention Socrates, or Theramenes, men distinguished by the glory of virtue and wisdom? When a certain Lacedæmonian, whose name is not so much as known, held death in such contempt, that, when led to it by the ephori, he looked cheerful and pleasant; and being thus interrupted by one of his enemies; "Do you despise the laws of Lycurgus?" he answered, "I am greatly obliged to him, for he has amerced me in a fine which I can pay without borrowing, or taking up at interest." This was a man worthy of Sparta! and I am almost persuaded of his innocency, from the greatness of his soul. Our city has produced many such. But why should I name generals, and other great men, when Cato could write, that legions have with alacrity marched to that place, from whence they never expected to return? With no less greatness of soul, fell the Lacedæmonians at Thermopylæ, of whom Simonides:

> Go, stranger, tell the Spartans, here we lie,
> Who to support their laws durst boldly die.

How nobly did Leonidas, their general, speak! "March on with courage, my Lacedæmonians; to-night, perhaps, we shall sup in the regions below." This was a brave nation, whilst the laws of Lycurgus were in force. One of them, when a Persian had said to him in conversation,

"We shall hide the sun by the number of our arrows and darts;" replied, "We shall fight then in the shade." Do I talk of their men? how great was that Lacedæmonian woman, who sent her son to battle, and hearing that he was slain, "I bore him," said she, "for that purpose, that you might have a man who durst die for his country."

XLIII. It is admitted that the Spartans were bold and hardy: the discipline of the republic greatly promoted this. What? have we not reason to admire Theodore, the Cyrenean, a philosopher of some distinction? who when Lysimachus threatened to crucify him, bid him keep those menaces for his courtiers: "Theodore is indifferent whether he rot in the air or underground." From which saying of the philosopher, an occasion is given me of speaking to the custom of burying and its ceremonies, which will require but few words, especially if we recollect what has been before said of the soul's insensibility. The opinion of Socrates in this is clear, from the book which treats of his death; of which we have already said a good deal; for when he had disputed about the immortality of the soul, and the time of his dying was near; being asked by Criton, how he would be buried; "I have taken a great deal of pains," saith he, "my friends, to no purpose, for I have not convinced our Criton, that I shall fly from hence, and leave no part of me behind? notwithstanding, Criton, if you can overtake me, wheresoever you get hold of me, bury me as you please: but believe me, none of you will be able to reach me when I fly hence." That was excellently said, for he allows his friend to do as he pleased, and yet shewed his indifference about any thing of this kind. Diogenes was something rougher, though of the same opinion; but as a Cynic, he expressed himself somewhat harsher; he ordered himself to be thrown any where without burying; when his friends replied, "What, to the birds and beasts?" "By no means," saith he, "place my staff near me, that I may drive them away." They answer, "How can you do that, for you will not perceive them?" "How am I concerned then in being torn by those animals, if I have no sense?" Anaxagoras, when he was near dying at Lampsacus, and was asked by his friends, whether, if any thing should happen to him, he would not choose to be carried to Clazomenæ, his country, made this excellent answer; "No," says he, "there is no occasion for that, all places are at an equal distance from the infernal regions." There is one thing to be observed on the whole of burying, that it relates to the body, whether the soul live or perish: now with regard to the body, it is clear, that, let the soul live or not, that has no sensation.

XLIV. But all things are full of errors. Achilles drags Hector, tied to his chariot; he thinks, I suppose, he tears his flesh, and that Hector feels the pain of it; therefore he is revenged, as he imagines; but Hecuba bewails this as a sore misfortune:

> I saw (a dreadful sight!) great Hector slain,
> Dragg'd at Achilles' car along the plain.

What Hector? or how long will he be Hector? Accius is better in this, and Achilles is sometimes more reasonable.

> I Hector's body to his sire convey'd,
> Hector I sent to the infernal shade.

It was not Hector that you dragged along, but a body that had been Hector's. Here another starts from underground, and will not suffer his mother to sleep;

To thee, I call, my once lov'd parent, hear,
Nor longer with thy sleep relieve thy care;
Thine eye unpitying me is clos'd—arise,
Ling'ring I wait the unpaid obsequies.

When these verses are sung with a slow and melancholy tune, so as to affect the whole theatre with sadness, one can scarce help thinking those unhappy, that are unburied:

Ere the devouring dogs and hungry vultures . . .

He is afraid he shall not have the use of his limbs so well, if they are torn to pieces, but is under no such apprehensions if they are burned:

Nor leave my naked bones, my poor remains,
To shameful violence, and bloody stains.

What could he fear, who could pour forth such excellent verses, to the sound of the flute? We must therefore adhere to this, that nothing is to be regarded after we are dead; though many revenge themselves on their dead enemies. Thyestes, in some good lines of Ennius, prays, first, that Atreus may perish by a shipwreck, which is certainly a very bad death; such an exit is very shocking! then follow these unmeaning expressions,

——May
On the sharp rock his mangled carcass lie,
His entrails torn, to hungry birds a prey,
May he convulsive writhe his pendant side,
And with his clotted gore the stones be dyed.

The stones had as much feeling as he who lay on them; though Thyestes imagines he has wished him the greatest torture: it would be pain indeed, were he sensible. But as he is not, it can be none: then how very unmeaning is this!

Let him, still hovering o'er the Stygian wave,
Ne'er reach the body's peaceful port, the grave.

You see what mistakes they are under; he imagines the body has its haven, and that the dead are at rest in their graves. Pelops was to blame not to have informed and taught his son what regard was due to every thing.

XLV. But there is no occasion to animadvert on the opinions of individuals, when you may observe whole nations to fall into those errors. The Egyptians embalmed their dead, and keep them in their houses; the Persians dress them over with wax, that they may preserve their bodies as long as possible. It is customary with the Magi, to bury none of their order, unless they have been first torn by dogs. In Hyrcania, the people maintain dogs for the public use, their nobles have their own: we know they have a good breed of dogs; but every one, according to his ability, provides himself with some, in order to be torn by them; and they hold that to be the best interment. Chrysippus, who is curious in all kinds of historical facts, has collected many other things of this kind, but some of them are so offensive as not to admit of being related. All that has been said of burying, is not worth our regard, with respect to ourselves, but not to be neglected as to our friends, provided we are persuaded that the dead are insensible: but the living indeed should consider what is due to custom and opinion, but they should in this consider too, that the dead are no ways interested in it. But death truly is then met with the greatest tranquillity, when the dying man can comfort himself with his own praise. No one dies too soon who has finished the course of perfect virtue. Death might have called on me often very seasonably; oh! how I wish it had! for I have gained nothing by the delay: I had gone over and over again the duties of life; nothing remained but to contend with fortune. If reason then cannot sufficiently fortify us to a contempt of death, let our past life confirm us in the conviction that we have lived too long: for, notwithstanding the deprivation of sense, the dead are not without that good which properly belongs to them, the praise and glory they have acquired, though they are not sensible of it. For although there be nothing in glory to make it desirable, yet it follows virtue as its shadow. But the judgment of the multitude on good men, if ever they form any, is more to their own praise, than of any real advantage to the dead; yet I cannot say, however it may be received, that Lycurgus and Solon are without the glory of their laws, and the public discipline they established: or that Themistocles and Epaminondas have not the glory of their martial virtue. Neptune shall sooner bury Salamine with his waters, than the memory of the trophies gained there; and the Bœotian Leuctra shall perish sooner, than the glory of that action. But the fame of Curius, Fabricius, Calatinus, the two Scipios, and the two Africani, Maximus, Marcellus, Paulus, Cato, Lælius, and numberless others, shall remain longer with them. Whoever has caught any resemblance of them, not estimating it by common fame, but the real applause of good men, may with confidence, should it be necessary, approach death; which we know to be, if not the chief good, at least no evil. Such a one would even choose to die, whilst he was in prosperity; for all the favours that could be heaped on him, would not be so agreeable to him, as to lose them, vexatious. That speech of the Lacedæmonian seems to have the same meaning; who, when Diagoras the Rhodian, who had himself been a conqueror at the Olympic games, saw two of his own sons conquerors there, he approached the old man, and congratulating him, said, "You should die now, Diagoras, for no greater happiness can attend you." The Greeks look on these as great things; perhaps they think too high of them, or rather did so then. He, who said this to Diagoras, looking on it as something very extraordinary, that three out of one family should have been conquerors there, thought it could answer no purpose to him, to continue any longer here, exposed only to a reverse of fortune.

XLVI. I might have given a satisfactory answer in this point, with few words, as you allowed the dead were not miserable: but I have laboured it the more for this reason, because this is our greatest consolation in the losing and bewailing of our friends. For we ought to bear with discretion any grief that arises from ourselves, or on our own account, lest we should seem to be influenced by self-love. But should we suspect our departed friends to be under those evils, which they are generally imagined to be, and to be sensible of them, such a suspicion would give us intolerable uneasiness: I wished, for my own sake, to pluck up this opinion by the root; and on that account I have been perhaps too tedious.

XLVII. *A.* You too tedious? no, indeed, not to me. I was induced by the former part of your speech, to wish to die; by the latter, to be indifferent, or at least not to be uneasy about it. But on the whole I am convinced that there can be no evil in death. *M.* Do you expect that I should give you an epilogue, like the rhetoricians, or shall I forego that art? *A.* I would not have you give over an art you have set off to such advantage; and you were in the right in that, for, to speak the truth, it has set you off. But what is that epilogue? for I should be glad to hear it, whatever it is. *M.* It is customary in the schools, to produce the opinions of the immortal gods on death; nor are these opinions the fruits of imagination alone, but have the authority of Herodotus and many others. Cleobis and Biton are the first they mention, sons of the Argive priestess; it is a known story. As it was necessary she should be drawn in a chariot, to a certain stated sacrifice, solemnized at a temple some considerable distance from the town, and the cattle that drew it went very slowly, those two young men I mentioned, pulling off their garments, and anointing their bodies with oil, applied themselves to the yoke. The priestess being thus conveyed to the temple drawn by her two sons, is said to have entreated the goddess to bestow on them, for their piety, the greatest gift that a god could confer: the young men, after having feasted with their mother, fell asleep; and in the morning they were found dead. Trophonius and Agamedes are said to have put up the same petition, who having built a temple to Apollo at Delphi, supplicating the god, desired of him some extraordinary reward for their care and labour, particularizing nothing, but only what was best for men. Apollo signified that he would bestow it the third day at sun-rising; on that day they were found dead. This they say was the particular determination of that god, to whom the rest of the deities have assigned the province of divining.

XLVIII. There is another little story told of Silenus, who, when taken prisoner by Midas, is said to have made him this present, for his ransom; he informed him, that never to have been born, was by far the greatest blessing that could happen to man; the nearest to it, was, to die very soon: which very opinion Euripides makes use of in his Cresphon,

> When man is born, 'tis fit, with solemn show,
> We speak our sense of his approaching woe;
> With other gestures, and a different eye,
> Proclaim our pleasure when he's bid to die.

There is something like this in Crantor's Consolation; for he saith, that Terinæus of Elysia, bemoaning heavily the loss of his son, came to a place of divination to be informed why he was visited with so great affliction, and received in his tablet these three verses:

> Thou fool, to murmur at Euthynous' death!
> The blooming youth to fate resigns his breath:
> That fate, whereon your happiness depends,
> At once the parent and the son befriends.

On these and such like authorities they affirm this cause to have been determined by the gods. But Alcidamas, an ancient rhetorician, of great reputation, wrote even in praise of death, by recounting the evils of life; he has much of the orator, but was unacquainted with the more refined arguments of the philosophers. With the rhetoricians indeed, to die for our country, is always not only glorious, but happy: they go back as far as Erectheus, whose very daughters underwent death, for the safety of their fellow-citizens: they instance Codrus, who threw himself into the midst of his enemies, dressed like a common man, that his royal robes might not betray him; because the oracle had declared the Athenians conquerors, if their king was slain. Menœceus is not overlooked by them, who, on the publishing of an oracle, freely gave up his blood to his country. Iphigenia ordered herself to be conveyed to Aulis, to be sacrificed, that her blood might be the means of spilling that of her enemies. From hence they proceed to instances of a fresher date. Harmodius and Aristogiton, Leonidas the Lacedæmonian, and Epaminondas the Theban, are much talked of; they were not acquainted with the many instances in our country, to give a list of whom would take up too much time; so great is the number of those to whom an honourable death was always desirable. Notwithstanding it is thus, we must use much persuasion, and a loftier strain of eloquence, to bring men to begin to wish to die, or to cease to be afraid of death. For if that last day doth not occasion an entire extinction, but a change of place only, what can be more desirable? but if it destroys, and absolutely puts an end to us, what is preferable to the having a deep sleep fall on us, in the midst of the fatigues of life, and thus overtaken to sleep to eternity? which, should it be the case, Ennius's speech exceeds Solon's; for our Ennius saith,

> Let none bestow upon my passing bier
> One needless sigh, or unavailing tear.

But that wise man,

> Let me not unlamented die, but o'er my bier
> Burst forth the tender sigh, the friendly tear.

Should it indeed be our case to know the time appointed by the gods for us to die, let us prepare ourselves for it, with a pleasant and grateful mind, as those who are delivered from a jail, and eased from their fetters, to go back to their eternal and (without dispute) their own habitation; or to be divested of all sense and trouble. But should we not be acquainted with this decree, yet should we be so disposed, as to look on that last hour as happy for us, though shocking to our friends; and never imagine that to be an evil, which is an appointment of the immortal gods, or of nature, the common parent of all. For it is not by hazard or without design that we have a being here; but doubtless there is a certain power, concerned for human nature; which would neither have produced nor provided for a being, which after having gone through the labours of life, was to fall into an eternal evil by death. Let us rather infer, that we have a retreat and haven prepared for us, which, I wish, we could make for, with crowded sails; but though the winds should not serve, yet we shall of course gain it, though somewhat later. But how can that be miserable for one which all must undergo? I have given you an epilogue, that you might not think I had overlooked or neglected any thing. *A.* I am persuaded you have not; and indeed that epilogue has confirmed me. *M.* I am glad it has had that effect; but it is now time to consult our healths; to-morrow, and all the time we continue here, let us consider this subject; and principally that which may ease our pain, alleviate our fears, and lessen our desires, which is the greatest advantage we can reap from the whole of philosophy.

BOOK II.

ON BEARING PAIN.

I. Neoptolemus in Ennius indeed saith, that the study of philosophy, moderately pursued, was expedient for him; but to give himself up entirely to it, was what he did not approve of. As to my part, Brutus, I am perfectly persuaded that it is expedient for me to philosophize; for what can I do better, having no employ? but I am not for proceeding but a little way in it, like him: for it is difficult to acquire the knowledge of a little, without acquainting yourself with many, or all its branches; nor can you well select that little but out of a great number: nor can any one who has acquired some knowledge thereof avoid endeavouring at more, with the same inclination. But in a life of business, like that of Neoptolemus, and in a military way, that little may have its use, and yield fruit, though uot so plentifully as the whole of philosophy; yet such as in some degree may at times lessen our desires, our sorrows, and our fears: just as the effect of our late Tusculan Disputations seemed to be a great contempt of death; which contempt is of no small efficacy to the ridding the mind of fear: for whoever dreads what cannot be avoided, can by no means live with any satisfaction. But he who is under no fear of death, not only from the necessity of dying, but from a persuasion that death itself hath nothing terrible in it, has very great security for a happy life. However, I am not ignorant, that many will strenuously oppose us; which can be no otherwise avoided than by not writing at all. For if my Orations, which were addressed to the judgment and approbation of the people, (for that is a popular art, and the effect of oratory is popular applause,) encountered some who are inclined to withhold their praise from every thing but what they are persuaded they can attain to themselves, and who confine good speaking to what they may hope to reach, and who declare, when they are overwhelmed with a flow of words and sentences, that they prefer the utmost poverty of thought and expression to that plenty and copiousness; (from whence arose the kind of Attic oratory, which they who professed it were strangers to, and which is already silenced, and laughed out of the very courts of justice;) what may I not expect, when at present I cannot have the least countenance from the people, by which I was upheld before? For philosophy is satisfied with a few judges, of herself industriously avoiding the multitude, who are jealous of it, and utterly displeased with it: so that, should any one undertake to cry down the whole, he would have the people on his side; or should he attack that, which I particularly profess, he might have assistance from the schools of the other philosophers. But I have answered the detractors of philosophy in general, in my Hortensius. What I had to say in favour of the Academics, is, I think, sufficiently explained in my Academics.

II. But yet I am so far from desiring that none should write against me, that it is what I most earnestly covet; for philosophy had never been in such esteem in Greece itself, but from the strength it acquired from the contentions and disputations of their learned men; therefore I recommend to all who have abilities, to snatch this art also from declining Greece, and transport it to us; as our ancestors by their study and industry imported all their other arts, which were worth having. Thus the praise of oratory, raised from a low degree, is arrived at such perfection, that it must now decline, and, as is the nature of all things, verge to its dissolution, in a very short time. Let philosophy then from this time spring afresh in the Latin tongue, and let us lend it our assistance, and let us bear patiently to be contradicted and refuted; which they dislike who are devoted to certain determined opinions, and are under such obligations to maintain them, that though they can support them by no arguments, they are forced to abide by them, to avoid the imputation of fickleness. We who pursue only probabilities, and cannot go beyond what is likely, can confute others without obstinacy, and are prepared to be confuted ourselves without resentment. Besides, were these studies brought home to us, we should not want Greek libraries, in which there is an infinite number of books, by reason of the multitude of authors among them; for it is a common practice with many to repeat the same things which have been wrote by others, which serves no purpose, but to stuff their shelves: and this will be our case, if many apply themselves to this study. But let us excite those, if possible, who have had a liberal education, and are masters of an elegant style, and philosophize with reason and method.

III. For there is a farther certain tribe who would willingly be called philosophers, whose books in our language are said to be numerous, which I do not despise, for indeed I never read them: but because the authors themselves declare that they write without any regularity or method, without elegance or ornament: I do not choose to read what is so void of entertainment. There is no one in the least acquainted with letters but knows the style and sentiments of that school; wherefore, since they are at no pains about expression, I do not see why they should be read by any but one another: let them read them, if they please, who are of the same opinions: for as all read Plato, and the other Socratics, with those who sprung from them, even they who do not allow of their opinions, or are very indifferent about them; but scarce any, except their own disciples, take Epicurus, or Metrodorus, into their hands; so they alone read these Latin books, who allow of their tenets. But, in my opinion, whatever is published, should be recommended to the reading of every man of learning; and though we may not succeed in this ourselves, yet nevertheless we must be sensible that this ought to be the aim of every writer. I am pleased with the manner of the Peripatetics, and Academics, of disputing on both sides of the question; not solely from its being the only method of discovering the probable, but because it affords the greatest scope for reasoning; a method that Aristotle first made use of, afterwards all the Aristotelians; and in our memory Philo, whom we have often heard, appointed one time to treat of the precepts of the rhetoricians, another for philosophy; to which custom I was brought to conform by means of my friends at my Tusculum, where our leisure time was spent in this manner. So that as we did yesterday, before noon we applied ourselves to speaking; and in the afternoon went down into the academy: the disputations held there I have acquainted you with, not in a narrative way, but almost in the same words in which they were carried on.

IV. The discourse then was introduced in this manner, whilst we were walking, and the exordium was somewhat thus. *A.* It is not to be expressed how much I was delighted, or rather edified, by your discourse of yesterday. Though I am conscious to myself that I was never over-fond of life, yet at times, when I have considered that there would be an end to this life, and that I must some time or other part with all its good things, a dread and uneasiness has intruded on my thoughts; but now, believe me, I am so freed from that kind of uneasiness, that I think it not worth any regard. *M.* I am not at all surprised at that, for it is the effect of philosophy, which is the medicine of our souls; it discharges all groundless apprehensions, frees us from desires, drives away fears: but it has not the same influence over all: it exerts itself most, when it falls in with a disposition proper for it. For fortune doth not alone, as the old proverb is, assist the bold, but reason more so; which, by certain precepts, as it were, confirms even courage itself. You were born naturally great and soaring, and with a contempt for all things here; therefore a discourse against death had an easy possession of a brave soul. But do you imagine that these same arguments have any force with those very persons who have invented, canvassed, and published them, excepting indeed some few particular persons? For how few philosophers will you meet with, whose life and manners are conformable to the dictates of reason? who look on their profession, not as a means of displaying their learning, but as a rule for their practice? who follow their own precepts, and comply with their own decrees? You may see some of that levity, that vanity, that it would have been better for them to have been ignorant; some covetous of money, some ambitious, many slaves to their lusts; so that their discourses and their actions are most strangely at variance; than which nothing in my opinion is more unbecoming; for it is just as if one who professed teaching grammar, should speak with impropriety; or a master of music sing out of tune; it has the worse appearance, because he acts contrary to his profession: so a philosopher, who errs in the conduct of his life, is the more infamous, because he mistakes in the very thing he pretends to teach, and whilst he lays down rules to regulate life by, is irregular in his own life.

V. *A.* Should this be the case, is it not to be feared that you are dressing up philosophy in false colours? for what stronger argument can there be, that it is of little use, than, that some complete philosophers live immorally? *M.* That indeed is no argument, for as all fields are not fruitful, because manured; and this sentiment of Accius is false, and asserted without any foundation,

> The ground you sow on, is of small avail;
> To yield a crop good seed can never fail:

so all minds do not answer their culture: and to go on with the comparison, as the field naturally fruitful cannot produce a crop, without dressing, so neither can the mind, without improvement; such is the weakness of either without the other. Whereas philosophy is the culture of the mind: this it is which plucks up vices by the roots; prepares the mind for the receiving of seed, commits them to it, or, as I may say, sows them, that, when come to maturity, they may produce a plentiful harvest. Let us proceed then as we begun; say, if you please, what shall be the subject of our disputation. *A.* I look on pain to be the greatest of all evils. *M.* What, greater than infamy? *A.* I dare not indeed assert that, and I blush to think I am so soon driven from my opinion. *M.* You would have had greater reason for blushing, had you persevered in it; for what is so unbecoming? what can appear worse to you, than disgrace, wickedness, immorality? To avoid which, what pain should we not only not refuse, but willingly take on ourselves? *A.* I am entirely of that opinion; but notwithstanding that pain is not the greatest evil, yet surely it is an evil. *M.* Do you perceive then how much of the terror of pain you have given up on a small hint? *A.* I see that plainly; but I should be glad to give up more of it. *M.* I will endeavour at it, but it is a great undertaking, and I must have no contradiction. *A.* You shall have none; as I behaved yesterday, so now I will follow reason wherever she leads.

VI. First, then, I will speak to the weakness of some, and the various sects of philosophers; the head of whom, both in authority and antiquity, was Aristippus, the Socratic, who hesitated not to say, that pain was the greatest of all evils. Next Epicurus easily gave in to this effeminate and enervated opinion. After him Hieronymus, the Rhodian, said, that to be without pain was the chief good, so great an evil did pain appear to him. The rest, excepting Zeno, Aristo, Pyrrho, were pretty much of the same opinion you were of just now, that it was indeed an evil, but there were many worse. Therefore what nature herself, and every generous soul disavows, that pain should be called the greatest of evils, and which you yourself renounced when infamy appeared in contrast to it, is this—what philosophy, the mistress of life, continues to maintain for so many ages. What duty of life, what praise, what reputation would be of such consequence, that a man should be desirous of gaining it at the expense of submitting to bodily pain, when he considers pain as the greatest evil? On the other side, what disgrace, what ignominy would he not submit to, that he might avoid pain, when persuaded that it was the greatest of evils? Besides, what person, who looks on pain as the greatest of evils, is not miserable, not only when he actually feels pain, but when he reflects that it may befall him? hence it follows that every man is miserable. Metrodorus indeed thinks him perfectly happy, whose body is free from all disorders, and has an assurance that it will always continue so; but who is there can be assured of that?

VII. Epicurus truly saith such things as if his design was to make people laugh; for he affirms somewhere, that if a wise man were to be burned, or put to the torture, you expect, perhaps, he should say that he would bear it, that he would support himself under it with resolution! (that, so help me, Hercules! would be very commendable, and becoming that very Hercules I adjured;) but this will not satisfy Epicurus, a robust and hardy man! No, if he were in Phalaris's bull, he would say, how sweet it is! how little do I regard it! What sweet? is it not sufficient, if it is not disagreeable? but those very men who deny pain to be an evil, to say that it is agreeable to any one to be tormented; they rather say, that it is hard, afflicting, unnatural, but yet no evil. He who saith it is the only evil, and the very worst of all evils, yet thinks a wise man would pronounce it sweet. I do not require of you to speak of pain in the same words which Epicurus doth, a man, as you know, devoted to pleasure; he may make no difference, if he pleases, between Phalaris's bull, and his own bed: but I cannot allow this wise man to be so indifferent about pain. If he bears it with courage, it is sufficient; that he should rejoice in it, I do not expect; for pain is certainly sharp, bitter, against nature, hard to submit to, and bear. Observe Philoctetes: we may allow him to lament, for he saw Hercules himself grieving loudly through extremity of pain on mount Œta: the arrows Hercules presented him with, were then no consolation to him, when

> The viper's bite, impregnating his veins
> With poison, rack'd him with its bitter pains.

And therefore he cries out, desiring help, and wishing to die,

> Oh! that some friendly hand its aid would lend,
> My body from this rock's vast height to send
> Into the briny deep! I'm all on fire,
> And by this fatal wound must soon expire.

It is hard to say, he was not oppressed with evil, and great evil too, who was obliged to cry out in this manner.

VIII. But let us observe Hercules himself, who was subdued by pain, at the very time he was in quest of immortality by dying. What words doth Sophocles here put in his mouth, in his Trachiniæ? who, when Deianira had put upon him a tunic dyed in the centaur's blood, and it stuck to his entrails, saith,

> What tortures I endure, no words can tell,
> Far greater these, than those which erst befel
> From the dire terror of thy consort, Jove;
> E'en stern Eurystheus' dire command above;
> This of thy daughter, Œneus, is the fruit,
> Beguiling me with her envenom'd suit,
> Whose close embrace doth on my entrails prey,
> Consuming life; my lungs forbid to play;
> The blood forsakes my veins, my manly heart
> Forgets to beat; enervated, each part
> Neglects its office, whilst my fatal doom
> Proceeds ignobly from the weaver's loom.
> The hand of foe ne'er hurt me, nor the fierce
> Giant, issuing from his parent earth.
> Ne'er could the Centaur such a blow enforce,
> No barbarous foe, nor all the Grecian force;

This arm no savage people could withstand,
Whose realms I travers'd, to reform the land.
Thus, though I ever bore a manly heart,
I fall a victim to a woman's art.
Assist, my son, if thou that name dost hear,
My groans preferring to thy mother's tear;
Convey her here, if, in thy pious heart,
Thy mother shares not an unequal part:
Proceed, be bold, thy father's fate bemoan,
Nations will join, you will not weep alone.
O what a sight is this same briny source,
Unknown before, through all my labours' course?
That virtue, which could brave each toil but late,
With woman's weakness now bewails its fate.
Approach, my son; behold thy father laid,
A wither'd carcase that implores thy aid;
Let all behold! and thou, imperious Jove,
On me direct thy lightning from above:
Now all its force the poison doth assume,
And my burnt entrails with its flame consume.
Crest-fallen, unembraced, I now let fall,
Listless, those hands that lately conquer'd all;
When the Nemæan lion own'd their force,
And he indignant fell a breathless corse:
The serpent slew, of the Lernean lake,
As did the Hydra of its force partake:
By this too fell the Erymanthian boar:
E'en Cerberus did his weak strength deplore.
This sinewy arm did overcome with ease
That dragon, guardian of the golden fleece.
My many conquests let some others trace;
It's mine to say, I never knew disgrace.

Can we then despise pain, when we see Hercules in such intolerable pain?

IX. Let us see what Æschylus says, who was not only a poet, but according to report a Pythagorean philosopher: how doth he make Prometheus bear the pain he suffered for the Lemnian theft, when he clandestinely stole away the celestial fire, and bestowed it on men, and was severely punished by Jupiter for the theft. Fastened to mount Caucasus, he speaks thus:

Thou heav'n-born race of Titans, here fast bound
Behold thy brother! As the sailors sound

With care the bottom, and their ships confine
To some safe shore, with anchor and with line.
So, by Jove's dread decree, the god of fire
Confines me here, the victim of Jove's ire.
With baneful art his dire machine he shapes;
From such a god what mortal e'er escapes?
When each third day shall triumph o'er the night,
Then doth the vulture with his talons light,
Seizing my entrails; which, in rav'nous guise,
He preys on! then with wings extended flies
Aloft, and brushes with his plumes the gore:
But when dire Jove my liver doth restore,
Back he returns impetuous to his prey;
Clapping his wings, he cuts th' etherial way.
Thus do I nourish with my blood this pest,
Confin'd my arms, unable to contest;
Intreating only, that in pity Jove
Would take my life, and this curs'd plague remove.
But endless ages past, unheard my moan,
Sooner shall drops dissolve this very stone.

We scarce think it possible not to call one affected in this manner, miserable; if such a one is miserable, then pain is an evil.

X. *A.* Hitherto you are on my side; I will see to that by and by; and, in the meanwhile, whence are those verses? I do not remember them. *M.* I will inform you, for you are in the right to ask; you see that I have much leisure. *A.* What then? *M.* I imagine, when you were at Athens, you attended frequently these schools? *A.* Yes, and with great pleasure. *M.* You observed then, though none of them at that time were very eloquent, yet they used to throw in verses in their harangues. *A.* Dionysius the Stoic used to apply a great many. *M.* You say right; but they were repeated without any choice or elegancy. But our Philo gave you a few select lines and well adapted; wherefore since I took a fancy to this kind of elderly declamation, I am very fond of quoting our poets, and where I cannot be supplied from them, I translate from the Greek, that the Latin language may want no ornament in this kind of disputation.

XI. But do you see the ill effects of poetry? The poets introduce the bravest men lamenting over their misfortunes: they soften our minds, and they are besides so entertaining, that we do not only read them, but get them by heart. Thus, what with poetry, our want of discipline at home, and our tender and delicate manner of living, virtue is become quite enervated. Plato therefore was right in banishing them his commonwealth, where he required the best morals, and the best form of government. But we, who have all our learning from Greece, read and learn these from our childhood; and look on this as a liberal and learned education.

XII. But why are we angry with the poets? we may find some philosophers, those masters of virtue, who taught that pain was the greatest of evils. But you, young man, when you said but just now that it appeared so to you, upon being asked, if greater than infamy, gave up that opinion at a word's speaking. Suppose I ask Epicurus the same question. He answers, that the least pain is a greater evil than the greatest infamy: that there is no evil in infamy itself, unless attended with pain. What pain then must attend Epicurus, when he saith this very thing, that pain is the greatest evil; for nothing can be a greater disgrace to a philosopher than to talk thus. Therefore you allowed enough, when you admitted infamy to appear to you a greater evil than pain. If you abide by this, you will see how far pain should be resisted: and that our inquiry should be, not so much whether pain be an evil, as how the mind may be fortified for resisting it. The Stoics infer from some trifling arguments, that it is no evil, as if the dispute was about a word, not the thing itself. Why do you impose upon me, Zeno? for when you deny, what appears very dreadful to me, to be an evil, I am deceived, and am at a loss to know why, what is to me so miserable, should be no evil. The answer is, that nothing is an evil but what is base and vicious. You return to your trifling, for you do not remove what made me uneasy. I know that pain is not vice, you need not inform me of that: but shew me, that, to be in pain or not, is all one; it has nothing to do, say you, with a happy life, for that consists of virtue alone; but yet pain is to be avoided. If I ask, why? it is disagreeable, against nature, hard to bear, woeful and afflicting.

XIII. Here are many words to express that variously, which we call by the single word, evil. You are defining pain, instead of removing it, when you say, it is disagreeable, unnatural, scarce to be borne: nor are you wrong in saying so, but the man who vaunts thus, and maintains nothing to be good but what is honest, nothing evil but what is base, should not give way to any pain. This would be wishing, not proving. This is better, and has more truth in it, that all things which nature abhors are to be looked on as evil; what she approves of, are to be considered as good: this admitted, and the dispute about words removed, that what they with reason embrace, and which we call honest, right, becoming, and sometimes include under the general name of virtue, would appear to such advantage, that all other things which are looked on as the gifts of fortune, or the good things of the body, would seem trifling and insignificant: no evil, nor all the collective body of evils together, would be comparable to the evil of infamy. Wherefore, if, as you granted in the beginning, infamy is worse than pain, pain is certainly nothing; for whilst it shall appear to you base and unmanly to groan, cry out, lament, or faint under pain, whilst you have any notion of probity, dignity, honour, and keeping your eye on them, you refrain yourself; pain will certainly yield to virtue, and by the influence of imagination will lose its whole force. For you must either give up virtue, or despise pain. Will you allow of such a virtue as prudence, without which no virtue can indeed be conceived? What then? will that suffer you to labour and take pains to no purpose? Will temperance permit you to do any thing to excess? Can justice be maintained by one, who through the force of pain betrays secrets, one that discovers his confederates, and relinquishes many duties of life? How will you act consistent with courage, and its attendants, greatness of soul, resolution, patience, a contempt for all worldly things? Can you hear yourself called a great man, when you lie groveling, dejected, and deploring yourself, with a lamentable voice; no one would call you a man, in such a condition: therefore you must either quit all pretensions to courage, or pain must be laid asleep.

XIV. You know very well, that though part of your Corinthian furniture be gone, the remainder is safe without that; but if you lose one virtue (though virtue cannot be lost); should you, I say, acknowledge that you were short in one, you would be stripped of all. Can you then call Prometheus a brave man, and of a great soul, endued with patience, and steadiness above the frowns of fortune? or Philoctetes, for I choose to instance in him, rather than yourself, for he certainly was not brave, who lay in his bed, watered with his tears,

> Whose groans, bewailings, and whose bitter cries,
> With grief incessant rend the very skies.

I do not deny pain to be pain; for were that the case, in what would courage consist? but I say it should be assuaged by patience, if there be such a thing as patience: if there be no such thing, why do we speak so in praise of philosophy? or why do we glory in its name? Pain vexes us, let it sting us to the heart; if you have no defence, submit to it; but if you are secured by Vulcanian armour, i. e. with resolution, oppose it; should you fail to do so, that guardian of your honour, your courage, would forsake and leave you. By the laws of Lycurgus, and by those which were given to the Cretans by Jupiter, or which Minos received from that god, as the poets say, the youths are trained up to hunting, running, enduring hunger and thirst, cold and heat. The boys at Sparta are scourged so at the altars, that the blood follows the lash, nay, sometimes, as I heard when I was there, they are whipped to death; and not one of them was ever heard to cry out, or so much as groan. What then? shall men not be able to bear what boys do? and shall custom have more force than reason?

XV. There is some difference betwixt labour and pain; they border upon one another, but with a distinction. Labour is a certain exercise of the mind or body, in some employ or undertaking that requires pains; but pain is a sharp motion in the body, disagreeable to our senses. Both these the Greeks, whose language is more copious than ours, express by the common name of *Πονος;* therefore they call industrious men, pains-taking, or rather fond of labour; we, more pertinently, laborious; for there is a difference betwixt labour and pain. You see, O Greece, your barrenness of words, sometimes, though you think you always abound. I say, then, there is a difference betwixt labour and pain. When Marius was cut for a swelling in his thigh, he felt pain; when he headed his troops in a very hot season, he laboured. Yet they bear some resemblance to one another; for the accustoming ourselves to labour makes us support pain with more ease. On this reason the founders of the Grecian form of government provided that the bodies of their youth should be strengthened by labour, which custom the Spartans transferred even to their women, who in other cities are more delicately clothed, and not exposed to the air: but it was otherwise with them.

> The Spartan women, with a manly air,
> Fatigues and dangers with their husbands share;
> They in fantastic sports have no delight,
> Partners with them in exercise and fight.

In these laborious exercises pain interferes sometimes, they are thrown down, receive blows, have bad falls and are bruised, and the labour itself hardens them against pain.

XVI. As to military service, (I speak of our own, not the Spartans', for they marched slow to the sound of the flute, and scarce a word of command was given without an anapest;) you may see whence the very name of an army (Exercitus) is derived; great is the labour of an army on its march; then consider that they carry more than a fortnight's provision, and whatever else they may want: then the burthen of the stakes, for as to shield, sword, or helmet, they look on them as no more incumbrance than their own limbs, for they say arms are the limbs of a soldier, which they carry so commodiously, that when there is occasion they throw down their burthens, and use their arms as readily as their limbs. What are the exercises of the legions? What labour in the running, encounters, shouts! Hence it is, that they make so slight of wounds in action. Take a soldier of equal bravery, but unexercised, and he will seem a woman; but why should there be this sensible difference betwixt a raw man, and an old soldier? It is true, the age of young soldiers is for the most part preferable, but it is practice that enables them to bear labour, and despise wounds. Thus you see, when the wounded are carried off the field, the raw untried soldier, though but slightly wounded, cries out most shamefully, but the more brave experienced veteran only inquires for some one to dress his wounds, and says,

> Patroclus, to thy aid I must appeal,
> Ere worse ensue, my bleeding wounds to heal;
> The sons of Æsculapius are employ'd,
> No room for me, so many are annoy'd.

XVII. This is certainly Eurypilus himself, experienced man!—Whilst his friend is continually enlarging on his sorrows, you may observe that he is so far from weeping, that he assigns a reason why he should bear his wounds with patience.

> Who at his enemy a stroke directs,
> His sword to light upon himself expects.

Patroclus, I imagine, were he a man, would lead him off to his chamber to bind up his wounds; but not a word of that, for he inquires how it went:

> Say how the Argives bear themselves in fight?

He could not express their toils so well by words, as what he had suffered himself:

> Peace! and my wounds bind up;

But though Eurypilus could not, Æsopus could.

> Where Hector's fortune press'd our yielding troops,

and he explains the rest, though in pain; so unbounded is military glory in a brave man! Cannot a wise and learned man achieve what this old soldier could? yes, indeed; and in a much better way; but at present I confine myself to custom and practice. I am not yet come to speak of reason and philosophy. You may often hear of diminutive old women living without victuals three or four days; but take away a wrestler's provision but for one day, he will implore Jupiter Olympius, the very god for whom he exercises himself: he will cry out, It is intolerable. Great is the force of custom! Sportsmen will continue whole nights in the snow: they will bear being parched upon the mountains. By custom the boxers will not so much as utter a groan, however bruised by the cestus. But what do you think of those who put a victory in the Olympics on a footing with the Consulate formerly? What wounds will the gladiators bear, who are either barbarians, or the dregs of men? How do they, who are trained to it, prefer being wounded to the basely avoiding it? How often do they appear to consider nothing but the giving satisfaction to their masters or the people? for when covered with wounds, they send to their masters to learn their pleasure; if it is their will, they are ready to lie down and die. What ordinary gladiator ever gave a sigh? Who ever turned pale? Who ever disgraced himself either on his legs, or when down? who that was on the ground ever drew in his neck to avoid the stroke? so great is the force of practice, deliberation, and custom! shall this then be done by

A Samnite rascal, worthy his employ?

And shall a man born to glory have so soft a part in his soul as not to be able to fortify himself by reason and reflection? The sight of the gladiator's combats is by some looked on as cruel and inhuman, and I do not know, as it is at present managed, but it may be so; but when the guilty fought, we might receive by our ears perhaps, by our eyes we could not, better instructions to harden us against pain and death.

XVIII. I have now done with exercise, custom, and a sense of honour; proceed we now to consider the force of reason, unless you have something to reply to what has been said. *A.* That I should interrupt you! by no means; for your discourse has brought me over to your opinion. *M.* It is the Stoics' business then to determine if pain be an evil or not, who endeavour to shew by some strained and trifling conclusions, which are nothing to the purpose, that pain is no evil. My opinion is, that whatever it is, it is not so great as it appears; and I say, that men are influenced more by some false representations and appearance of it, and that all which is really felt is tolerable. Where shall I begin then? shall I superficially go over what I said before, that my discourse may have a greater scope?

This then is agreed on by all, both by the learned and unlearned, that it becomes the brave and magnanimous, those that have patience and a spirit above this world, not to give way to pain; and every one commends a man who bears it thus. Whatever then is expected from a brave man, and is commendable in him, it would be base in any one to be afraid of at its approach, or not to bear when it came. But I would have you be aware, that all the right affections of the soul come under the name of virtues; this is not properly the name of them all, but that they all have their name from some leading virtue: for virtue comes from *vir* the Latin name of a man, and courage is the peculiar distinction of a man. Now there are two distinct offices in this, a contempt of death, and of pain. We must then provide ourselves with these; if we would be men of virtue, or rather, if we would be men, because virtue takes its very name from *vir*, i. e. man.

XIX. You may inquire perhaps how? and such an inquiry is not amiss, for philosophy is ready with her assistance. Epicurus offers himself to you, far from a bad man, or rather a very good one; he advises no more than he knows; Despise, saith he, pain. Who is it saith this? the same who calls pain the greatest of all evils, not very consistently indeed. Let us hear him. If the pain is at the height, it must needs be short. I must have that over again, for I do not apprehend what you mean by at the height or short. That is at the height, than which nothing is higher; that is short, than which nothing is shorter. I do not regard the greatness of any pain, from which, by the shortness of its continuance, I shall be delivered almost before it reaches me. But if the pain be as great as that of Philoctetes, it will appear great indeed to me, but yet not the greatest I am capable of; for the pain is confined to my foot: but my eye may pain me, I may have a pain in the head, sides, lungs, every part of me. It is far then from being at the height; therefore, says he, pain of a long continuance has more pleasure in it than uneasiness. Now I cannot bring myself to say, so great a man talks nonsense, but I imagine he laughs at us. My opinion is, that the greatest pain (I say, the greatest, though it may be ten atoms less than another) is not therefore short because acute; I could name you a great many good men who have been tormented many years with the acutest pains of the gout. But this cautious man doth not determine the measure of that greatness; nor, as I know, doth he fix what he means by great with regard to the pain, nor short with respect to its continuance. Let us pass him by then as one who says just nothing at all; and let us force him to acknowledge, notwithstanding he might behave himself somewhat boldly under his colic and his strangury, that no remedy against pain can be had from him who looks on pain as the greatest of all evils. We must apply then for relief elsewhere, and no where better to all appearance than from those who place the chief good in honesty, and the greatest evil in infamy. You dare not so much as groan, or discover the least uneasiness in their company, for virtue itself speaks to you through them.

XX. Will you, when you may observe children at Lacedæmon, young men at Olympia, Barbarians in the amphitheatre, receive deep wounds, and never once open their mouths; will you, I say, when any pain twitches you, cry out like a woman? should you not rather bear it with resolution and constancy? and not cry, It is intolerable, nature cannot bear it. I hear what you say, boys bear this, led thereto by glory: some bear it through shame, many through fear; and do we imagine that nature cannot bear what is borne by many, and in such different circumstances? nature not only bears it, but challenges it, for there is nothing with her preferable to it, nothing she desires more than credit and reputation, than praise, than honour, and glory. I was desirous of describing this under many names, and I have used many, that you may have the clearer idea of it; for I meant to say, that whatever is desirable of itself, proceeding from virtue, or placed in virtue, and commendable on its own account, (which I should sooner call the only good than the chief good,) is what men should prefer above all things. As we declare thus of honesty, the contrary is due to infamy: nothing is so odious, so detestable, nothing so unworthy a man, which if you are convinced of, (for at the beginning of this discourse you allowed, that there appeared to you more evil in infamy than pain,) what remains is, that you have the command over yourself.

XXI. Though the expression may not seem justifiable to bid you divide yourself, assign to one part of man command, to the other submission, yet it is not without its elegancy. For the soul admits of a two-fold division, one of which partakes of reason, the other is without it; when therefore we are ordered to give a law to ourselves, the meaning is, that reason should restrain our rashness. Every soul of man has naturally something soft, low, enervated in a manner, and languid. Were there nothing besides this, men would be the greatest of monsters; but there is present to every man reason, which presides and gives law to all, which by improving itself, and making continual advances, becomes perfect virtue. It behoves a man then to take care, that reason has the command over that part to which obedience is assigned; as a master over his slave, a general over his army, a father over his son. If that part of the soul misbehaves, which I call soft, if it gives itself up to lamentations, and womanish tears, it should be restrained, and committed to the care of friends and relations, for we often see those brought to order by shame, whom no reasons can affect. Therefore we should confine those like our servants, in safe custody, with chains. But those who have more resolution, yet are not so stout as they should be, we should encourage with our advice, to behave as good soldiers, recollecting themselves to maintain their honour. That wise man at Greece, in the Niptræ, doth not lament too much over his wounds, or rather he is moderate in his grief:

> Move slow, my friends, your hasty speed refrain,
> Lest by your motion you increase my pain.

Pacuvius is better in this than Sophocles, for with him Ulysses bemoans his wounds too lamentably; for the very people who carried him after he was wounded, though his grief was moderate, yet considering the dignity of the man, did not scruple to say,

> E'en thou, Ulysses, long to war inur'd,
> Thy wounds, though great, too feebly hast endur'd.

The wise poet understood that custom was no contemptible instructor how to bear pain. But the same complains with more decency, though in great pain,

> Assist, support me, never leave me so;
> Unbind my wounds; oh! execrable woe!

He begins to give way, but instantly checks himself.

> Away, begone, but cover first the sore;
> For your rude hands but make my pains the more.

Do you observe how he constrains himself, not that his bodily pains were less, but he corrects the sense of them? Therefore in the conclusion of the Niptræ he blames others, even when he was dying.

> Complaint on fortune may become the man,
> None but a woman will thus weeping stand.

That soft place in his soul obeys his reason, as an abashed soldier doth his stern commander.

XXII. Whenever a completely wise man shall appear, (such indeed, we have never as yet seen, but the philosophers have described, in their writings, what sort of man he is to be, if ever he is); such an one, or at least his perfect reason, will have the same authority over the inferior part as a good parent has over his dutiful children, he will bring it to obey his nod, without any trouble or pains. He will rouse himself, prepare and arm himself to oppose pain as he would an enemy. If you inquire what arms he will provide himself with; he will struggle with his pain, assume a resolution, will reason with himself; he will say thus to himself, Take care that you are guilty of nothing base, languid, or unmanly. He will turn over in his mind all the different kinds of honesty. Zeno of Elea will be presented to him, who suffered every thing rather than betray his confederates in the design of putting an end to the tyranny. He will reflect on Anaxarchus, the Democritian, who having fallen into the hands of Nicocreon king of Cyprus, without the least entreaty or refusal submitted to every kind of torture. Calanus, the Indian, will occur to him, an ignorant man, and a barbarian, born at the foot of Mount Caucasus, who committed himself to the flames by a free voluntary act. But we, if we have the tooth-ache, or a pain in the foot, or if the body be any ways affected, cannot bear it. Our sentiments of pain, as well as pleasure, are so trifling and effeminate, we are so enervated and dissolved, that we cannot bear the sting of a bee without crying out. But C. Marius, a plain countryman, but of a manly soul, when he was cut, as I mentioned above, at first refused to be tied down, and he is the first instance of any one's being cut without tying down: why did others bear this afterwards from the force of example? You see then pain is more in opinion than nature, and yet the same Marius is a proof that there is something very sharp in pain, for he would not submit to have the other thigh cut. So that he bore his pain with resolution; but as a man, he was not willing to undergo any greater without evident cause. The whole then consists in this, to have the command over yourself: I have already told you what kind of command this is, and by considering what is most consistent with patience, fortitude, and greatness of soul, a man not only refrains himself, but by some means or other even mitigates pain itself.

XXIII. Even as in a battle, the dastardly and timorous soldier throws away his shield on the first appearance of an enemy, and runs as fast as he can, and on that account loses his life sometimes, though his body is never touched, when he who stands his ground meets with nothing like this: so, they who cannot bear the appearances of pain, throw themselves away, and give themselves up to affliction and dismay. But they that oppose it, are often more than a match for it. For the body has a certain resemblance to the soul: as burdens are the easier borne the more the body is exerted, and they crush us if we give way; so the soul by exerting itself resists the whole weight that would oppress it; but if it yields, it is so pressed, that it cannot support itself. And if we consider things truly, the soul should exert itself in every pursuit, for that is the only security for its doing its duty. But this should be principally regarded in pain, not to do any thing timidly, dastardly, basely, slavishly, or effeminately, and above all things we should dismiss and discharge that Philoctetean clamour. A man is allowed sometimes to groan, but yet seldom, but it is not sufferable even in a woman to howl; and this is the very funeral lamentation which is forbidden by the twelve tables. Nor doth a wise or brave man ever groan, unless when he exerts himself to give his resolution greater force, as they that run in the stadium, make as much noise as they can. It is the same with the wrestlers; but the boxers, when they aim a blow with the cestus at their adversary, give a groan, not because they are in pain, or from a sinking of their spirits, but because their whole body is upon the stretch when they throw out these groans, and the blow comes the stronger.

XXIV. What! they who would speak louder than ordinary, are they satisfied with working their jaws, sides, or tongue, or stretching the common organs of speech? the whole body is at full stretch, if I may be allowed the expression, every nerve is exerted to assist their voice. I have actually seen M. Antony's knee touch the ground when he was speaking with vehemence for himself, with relation to the Varian law. As the engines you throw stones or darts with, throw them out with the greater force the more they are strained and drawn back, so it is in speaking, running, or boxing, the more people strain themselves, the greater their force. Since therefore this exertion has so much attributed to it, we should apply it in pain, if it helps to strengthen the mind. But if it is a groan of lamentation, if it is weakness or abjectness; I should scarce call him a man who complied with it. For even supposing that such groaning give any ease, it should be considered, whether it was consistent with a brave and resolute man. But, if it doth not ease our pain, why should we debase ourselves to no purpose? for what is more unbecoming in a man than to cry like a woman? But this precept about pain is not confined to that; we should apply this exertion of the soul to every thing else. Doth anger, rage, or lust prevail? We should have recourse to the same magazine, and apply to the same arms; but since our subject is pain, we will let the others alone. To bear pain then sedately and calmly, it is of great use to consider with all our soul, as the saying is, how noble it is to do so, for we are naturally desirous (as I said before, nor can it be too often repeated) and very much inclined to what is honest, of which if we discover but the least glimpse, there is nothing we are not prepared to undergo and suffer to attain it. From this impulse of our minds, this tendency to true praise and honesty, such dangers are supported in war, brave men are not sensible of their wounds in action, or if they are sensible, prefer death to the departing but the least step from their honour. The Decii saw the shining swords of their enemies when they rushed into the battle. The dying nobly, and the glory, made all fear of death of little weight. Do you imagine that Epaminondas groaned when he perceived that his life flowed out with his blood? for he left his country triumphing over the Lacedæmonians, whereas he found it in subjection to them. These are the comforts, these are the things that assuage the greatest pain.

XXV. You may ask, how the case is in peace? what is to be done at home? how we are to behave in bed? You bring me back to the philosophers, who seldom go to war. Among these, Dionysius of Heraclea, a man certainly of no resolution, having learned the bravery of Zeno, quitted it on being in pain: for being tormented with a pain in his kidneys, in bewailing himself he cried out, that those things were false which he had formerly conceived of pain. Who, when his fellow-disciple Cleanthes asked him why he had changed his opinion, answered, Whoever had applied so much time to philosophy, and cannot bear pain, may be a sufficient proof that pain is an evil. I have spent many years at philosophy, and yet cannot bear pain. Pain is therefore an evil. It is reported that Cleanthes on that struck his foot on the ground, and repeated a verse out of the Epigonæ:

Amphiaraus, hear'st thou this below?

He meant Zeno: he was sorry the other degenerated from him.

But it was not so with our Posidonius, whom I have often seen myself, and I will tell you what Pompey used to say of him; that when he came to Rhodes, on his leaving Syria, he had great desire to hear Posidonius, but was informed that he was very ill of a severe fit of the gout: yet he had great inclination to pay a visit to so famous a philosopher. When he had seen him, and paid his compliments, and had spoken with great respect of him, he said he was very sorry that he could not have a lecture from him. But, indeed you may, replied the other, nor will I suffer any bodily pain to occasion so great a man to visit me in vain. On this Pompey relates, that as he lay on his bed, he disputed gravely and copiously on this very subject, that nothing was good but what was honest: that in his paroxysms he would often say, Pain, it is to no purpose, notwithstanding you are troublesome, I will never acknowledge you an evil: and in general all honourable and illustrious labours become tolerable by disregarding them.

XXVI. Do we not observe, that where those exercises called gymnastic are in esteem, those who enter the lists never concern themselves about dangers? where the praise of riding and hunting prevails, they who pursue this decline no pain? What shall I say of our own ambitious pursuits, or desire of honour? What fire will not candidates run through to gain a single vote? Therefore Africanus had always in his hand the Socratic Xenophon, being particularly pleased with his saying, that the same labours were not equally heavy to the general and to the common man, because honour itself made the labour lighter to the general. But yet, so it happens, that even with the illiterate vulgar, an opinion of honour prevails, though they cannot discern what it is. They are led by report and common opinion to look on that as honourable, which has the general voice. Not that I would have you, should the multitude be ever so fond of you, rely on their judgment, nor approve of what they think right; you must use your own judgment. Should you have a pleasure in approving what is right, you will not only have the mastery over yourself, (which I recommended to you just now,) but over every body, and every thing. Lay this down then, that a great capacity, and most lofty elevation of soul, which distinguishes itself most by despising and looking down with contempt on pain, is the most excellent of all things, and the more so, if it doth not depend on the people, nor aims at applause, but derives its satisfaction from itself. Besides, to me indeed every thing seems the more commendable, the less the people are courted, and the fewer eyes there are to see it. Not that you should avoid the public, for every generous action loves the public view; yet no theatre for virtue is equal to a consciousness of it.

XXVII. And let this be principally considered, that this bearing of pain, which I have often said is to be strengthened by an exertion of the soul, should be the same in every thing. For you meet with many who, through a desire of victory, or for glory, or to maintain their rights, or their liberty, have boldly received wounds, and bore themselves up under them; and the very same persons, by remitting from that intenseness of their minds, were unequal to bearing the pain of a disease. For they did not support themselves under their sufferings by reason or philosophy, but by inclination and glory. Therefore some barbarians and savage people are able to fight very stoutly with the sword, but cannot bear sickness like men: but the Grecians, men of no great courage, but as wise as human nature will admit of, cannot look an enemy in the face, yet the same will bear to be visited with sickness tolerably, and manly enough; and the Cimbrians and Celtiberians are very alert in battle, but bemoan themselves in sickness; for nothing can be consistent which has not reason for its foundation. But when you see those who are led by inclination or opinion, not retarded by pain in their pursuits, nor hindered from obtaining them, you should conclude, either that pain is no evil, or that, notwithstanding whatever is disagreeable, and contrary to nature, you may choose to call an evil, yet it is so very small, that it may so effectually be got the better of by virtue as quite to disappear. Which I would have you think of night and day; for this argument will spread itself and take up more room sometime or other, and not be confined to pain alone; for if the motives to all our actions are to avoid disgrace and acquire honour, we may not only despise the stings of pain, but the storms of fortune, especially if we have recourse to that retreat which was our yesterday's subject. As, if some god had advised one who was pursued by pirates, to throw himself overboard, saying, there is something at hand to receive you, either a dolphin will take you up as it did Arion of Methymna, or those horses sent by Neptune to Pelops (who are said to have carried chariots so rapidly as to be borne up by the waves) will receive you, and convey you wherever you please, he would forego all fear: so, though your pains be ever so sharp and disagreeable, if they are not so great as to be intolerable, you see where you may betake yourself. I thought this would do for the present. But perhaps you still abide by your opinion. *A.* Not in the least, indeed; and I hope I am freed by these two days' discourses from the fear of two things that I greatly dreaded. *M.* To-morrow then for rhetoric, as we were saying, but I see we must not drop our philosophy. *A.* No, indeed, we will have the one in the forenoon, this at the usual time. *M.* It shall be so, and I will comply with your very laudable inclinations.

BOOK III.

ON GRIEF OF MIND.

WHAT reason shall I assign, Brutus, why, as we consist of soul and body, the art of curing and preserving the body should be so much sought after, and the invention of it, as being so useful, should be ascribed to the immortal gods; but the medicine of the soul should neither be the object of inquiry, whilst it was unknown, nor so much improved after its discovery, nor so well received or approved of by some, disagreeable, and looked on with an envious eye by many others? Is it because the soul judges of the pains and disorders of the body, but we do not form any judgment of the soul by the body? Hence it comes that the soul never judgeth of itself, but when that by which itself is judged is in a bad state. Had nature given us faculties for discerning and viewing herself, and could we go through life by keeping our eye on her, our best guide, no one certainly would be in want of philosophy or learning. But, as it is, she has furnished us only with some few sparks, which we soon so extinguish by bad morals and depraved customs, that the light of nature is quite put out. The seeds of virtues are connatural to our constitutions, and were they suffered to come to maturity, would naturally conduct us to a happy life; but now, as soon as we are born and received into the world, we are instantly familiarized to all kinds of depravity and wrong opinions; so that we may be said almost to suck in error with our nurse's milk. When we return to our parents, and are put into the hands of tutors and governors, we imbibe so many errors, that truth gives place to falsehood, and nature herself to established opinion. To these we may add the poets; who, on account of the appearance they exhibit of learning and wisdom, are heard, read, and got by heart, and make a deep impression on our minds. But when to these are added the people, who are as it were one great body of instructors, and the multitude, who declare unanimously for vice, then are we altogether overwhelmed with bad opinions, and revolt entirely from nature; so that they seem to deprive us of our best guide, who have ascribed all greatness, worth, and excellence, to honour, and power, and popular glory, which indeed every excellent man aims at; but whilst he pursues that only true honour, which nature has in view, he finds himself busied in arrant trifles, and in pursuit of no conspicuous form of virtue, but a shadowy representation of glory. For glory is a real and express substance, not a mere shadow. It consists in the united praise of good men, the free voice of those who form true judgments of pre-eminent virtue; it is as it were the very echo of virtue; which being generally the attendant on laudable actions, should not be slighted by good men. But popular fame, which would pretend to imitate it, is hasty and inconsiderate, and generally commends wicked and immoral actions, and taints the appearance and beauty of the other, by assuming the resemblance of honesty. By not being able to discover the difference of these, some men, ignorant of real excellence, and in what it consists, have been the destruction of their country or of themselves. And thus the best men have erred, not so much in their intentions, as by a mistaken conduct. What, is there no cure for those who are carried away by the love of money, or the lust of pleasures, by which they are little short of madmen, which is the case of all weak people? or is it because the disorders of the mind are less dangerous than those of the body? or because the body will admit of a cure, but the soul is incurable?

III. But there are more disorders of the mind than of the body, for the generality, and of a more dangerous nature; for these very disorders are the more offensive, because they belong to the mind, and disturb that; and the mind, when disordered, is, as Ennius saith, in a constant error; it can neither bear nor endure any thing, and is under the perpetual influence of desires. Now what disorders can be worse to the body than these two distempers of the mind, (for I overlook others,) weakness, and desires? But how indeed can it be maintained that the soul cannot prescribe to itself, when she invented the very medicine for the body; when, with regard to bodily cures, constitution and nature have a great share; nor do all, who suffer themselves to be cured, find instantly that effect; but those minds which are disposed to be cured, and submit to the precepts of the wise, may undoubtedly recover a healthy state? Philosophy is certainly the medicine of the soul; whose assistance we do not seek from abroad, as in bodily disorders, neither are we ourselves obliged to exert our utmost abilities in order to our cure. But as to philosophy in general, I have, I think, in my *Hortensius* sufficiently spoken of the credit and improvement it deserves: since that, indeed, I have continually either disputed or written on its most material branches: and I have laid down in these books what I disputed with my particular friends at my Tusculum: but as I have spoken in the two former of pain and death, the third day of our disputation shall make up this volume. When we came down into the academy, the day declining towards afternoon, I asked of one of those who were present a subject to discourse on; then the business was carried on in this manner.

IV. *A.* My opinion is, that a wise man is subject to grief. *M.* What, and to the other perturbations of mind, as fears, lusts, anger? For these are pretty much like what the Greeks call παθη. I might name them diseases, and that would be literal, but it is not agreeable to our way of speaking. For envy, delight, and pleasure, are all called by the Greeks diseases, being motions of the mind repugnant to reason: but we, I think, are right, in calling the same motions of a disturbed soul, perturbations, very seldom diseases; unless it appears otherwise to you. *A.* I am of your opinion. *M.* And do you think a wise man subject to these? *A.* Entirely, I think. *M.* Then that boasted wisdom is but of small account, if it differs so little from madness. *A.* What? doth every commotion of the mind seem to you to be madness? *M.* Not to me only; but I apprehend, though I have often been surprised at it, that it appeared so to our ancestors many ages before Socrates: from whom is derived all that philosophy which relates to life and morals. *A.* How so? *M.* Because the name madness implies a sickness of the mind and disease, that is an unsoundness, and a distemperature of mind, which they call madness. The philosophers called all perturbations of the soul diseases, and their opinion was, that no fool was free from these; but all that are diseased are unsound, and the minds of all fools are diseased, therefore all fools are mad. They held a soundness of the mind to depend on a certain tranquillity and steadiness; they called that madness, where the mind was without these, because soundness was inconsistent with a perturbed mind, as well as a disordered body.

V. Nor were they less ingenious in calling the state of the soul, devoid of the light of reason, "out of itself," i. e. mad. From whence we may understand, that they who gave these names to things were of the same opinion with Socrates, that all silly people were unsound, which the Stoics, as received from him, have carefully preserved; for whatever mind is distempered, (and as I just now said, the philosophers call all perturbed motions of the mind distempers,) is no more sound than a body in a fit of sickness. Hence it is, that wisdom is the soundness of the mind, folly the distempered state, which is unsoundness, and that is madness; and these are much better expressed by the Latin words than the Greek: which you will find in many other places. But of that elsewhere: now, to our present purpose. The very force of the word speaks what, and what kind of thing it is we inquire after. For we must necessarily understand by the sound, those whose minds are under no perturbation from any motion, as it were a disease. They who are differently affected we must necessarily call unsound. So that nothing is better than what is usual in Latin, to say, that they who are run away with by their lust or anger, have quitted the command over themselves; though anger includes lust, for anger is defined to be the lust of revenge. They then who are said not to be masters of themselves, are said to be so, because they are not under the government of reason, to which is assigned by nature the power over the whole soul. Why the Greeks should call this μανια, I do not easily apprehend; but we define it much better than they, for we distinguish this madness, which, being allied to folly, is more extensive, from what is called a *furor*, or raving. The Greeks indeed would do so too, but they have no one word that will express it; what we call *furor*, they call μελαγχολια, as if the reason were affected only by a black bile, and not disturbed as often by a violent rage, or fear, or grief. Thus we say Athamas, Alcmæon, Ajax, and Orestes, were raving; because one affected in this manner was not allowed by the twelve tables to have the management of his own affairs; therefore the words are not, if he is mad, but, if he begins to be raving. For they look upon madness to be an unsettled humour, that proceeded from not being of sound mind: yet such a one might take care of common things, execute the usual and customary duties of life: but they thought one that was raving to be totally blind; which notwithstanding it is allowed to be greater than madness, is nevertheless of such a nature, that a wise man may be even subject to raving. But this is another question: we will return to our purpose.

VI. I think you said that it was your opinion, a wise man was subject to grief. And so indeed I think. *M.* It is natural enough to think so, for we are not the offspring of a rock: but we have by nature something soft and tender in our souls, which may be put into a violent motion by grief, as by a storm; nor did that Crantor, who was one of the most distinguished of our academy, say this amiss: "I am by no means of their opinion, who talk so much in praise of I know not what insensibility, which neither can be, nor ought to be: I would choose," saith he, "never to be ill; but should I be so, I should choose to have my feeling, either supposing there was to be an amputation, or any other separation of my body. For that insensibility cannot be but at the expense of some unnatural wildness of mind, or stupor of body." But let us consider if to talk thus is not allowing that we are weak, and complying with our softness. Notwithstanding, let us be hardy enough, not only to lop off every arm of our miseries, but pluck up every fibre of their roots: yet still something perhaps may be left behind, so deep doth folly strike its roots: but whatever may be left, it should be no more than is necessary. But let us be persuaded of this, that unless the mind be in a sound state, which philosophy alone can effect, there can be no end of our miseries. Wherefore, as we begun, let us submit ourselves to it for a cure; we may be cured if we please. I shall advance something farther. I shall not treat of grief alone, though that indeed is the principal thing; but, as I proposed, of every disorder of the mind, as the Greeks call it: and first, with your leave, I shall treat it in the manner of the Stoics, whose method is to reduce their arguments into a little room: then I shall enlarge more in my own way.

VII. A man of courage relies on himself; I do not say is confident, because by a bad custom of speaking that is looked on as a fault, though the word is derived from confiding in yourself, which is commendable. He who relies on himself, is certainly under no fear; for there is a repugnance betwixt this self-reliance and fear. Now whoever is subject to grief is subject to fear; for whatever things we grieve at when present, we dread as hanging over us and approaching. Thus it comes about, that grief is repugnant to courage: it is very probable, therefore, that whoever is subject to grief, the same is liable to fear, and a kind of broken-heartedness and sinking. Now whenever these befall a man, he is in a servile state, and must own that he is overpowered. Whoever entertains these, must entertain timidity and cowardice. But these cannot befall a man of courage; neither therefore can grief; but the man of courage is the only wise man: therefore grief cannot befall the wise man. It is besides necessary, that whoever is brave, should be a man of a great soul; a great soul is invincible: whoever is invincible looks down with contempt on all things here, and holds them as below him. But no one can despise those things on account of which he may be affected with grief: from whence it follows, that a wise man is never affected with grief, for all wise men are brave, therefore a wise man is not subject to grief. As the eye, when disordered, is not in a disposition for performing its office well; and the other parts, with the body itself, when dislocated, cannot perform their office and appointment; so the mind, when disordered, is ill disposed to do its duty: the office of the mind is to use its reason well; but the mind of a wise man is always in condition to make the best use of his reason, therefore is never out of order. But grief is a disorder of the mind, therefore a wise man will be always free from it.

VIII. It is very probable, that what the Greeks mean by their *Σωφρονα*, is the temperate man with us, for they call all that virtue *Σωφροσυνην*, which I one while name temperance, at another time moderation, nay sometimes modesty; and I do not know whether that virtue may not be properly called frugality, which has a more confined meaning with the Greeks; for they call frugal men *χρησιμους*, which implies only that they are useful: but it has a more extensive meaning; for all abstinence, all innocency, (which the Greeks have no common name for, though they might have *ἀβλάβειαν*, for innocency is that affection of mind which would offend no one,) and several other virtues, are comprehended under frugality, which, were it not of the first rate, but confined into so small a compass as some imagine, the surname of Piso would not have been in so great esteem. But as we allow him not the name of a frugal man *(frugi)*, who either quits his post through fear, which is cowardice; or who reserves to his own use what was privately committed to his keeping, which is injustice; or who misbehaves through rashness, which is folly; for that reason the word frugality takes in these three virtues of fortitude, justice, and prudence, though this is common with all virtues, for they are all connected and knit together. Let us allow then frugality to be the other and fourth virtue; the peculiar property of which seems to be, to govern and appease all tendencies to too eager a desire after any thing, to refrain lust, and preserve a decent steadiness in every thing. The vice in contrast to this, is called prodigality. Frugality I imagine is derived from fruits, the best thing the earth produces. Whoever is frugal then, or if it is more agreeable to you, whoever is moderate, temperate, such a one must of course be constant; whoever is constant, must be quiet: the quiet man must be void of all perturbation, therefore of grief likewise: and these are the properties of a wise man; therefore a wise man must be without grief.

IX. So that Dionysius of Heraclea is right when, upon this complaint of Achilles in Homer,

> Anger and rage my breast inflame,
> My glory tarnished, and since lost my fame,

he reasons thus: Is the hand as it should be, when it is affected with a swelling, or is any other member of the body when it is not in its natural state? Must not the mind then, when it is puffed up, or distended, be out of order? But the mind of a wise man is without any disorder; it never swells, or is puffed up; but the mind in anger is otherwise. A wise man therefore is never angry; for when he is angry, he lusts after something, for whoever is angry naturally has a longing desire to give all the pain he can to the person he thinks has injured him; but whoever has this earnest desire must necessarily be much pleased with the accomplishment of his wishes; hence he is delighted with his neighbour's misery; which as a wise man is not capable of, he is not capable of anger. But should a wise man be subject to grief, he may likewise be subject to anger, from which being free, he must be void of grief. Besides, could a wise man be subject to grief, he might be so to pity, he might be open to a disposition for envy: I do not say he might be envious, for that consists of the very act of envying.

X. Therefore compassion and envy are consistent in the same man; for whoever is uneasy at any one's adversity, is uneasy at another's prosperity: as Theophrastus laments the loss of his companion Callisthenes, and is disturbed at the success of Alexander; therefore he saith, that Callisthenes met with a man of great power and success, but who did not know how to make use of his good fortune; and as pity is an uneasiness arising from the misfortunes of another, so envy is an uneasiness that proceeds from the good success of another: therefore whoever is capable of pity, is capable of envy. But a wise man is incapable of envy, and consequently of pity. For were a man used to grieve, to pity would be familiar to him; therefore to grieve is far from a wise man. Though these reasonings of the Stoics, and their conclusions, are rather stiff and contracted, and require a more diffuse and free way, yet great stress is to be laid on the opinions of those men, who have a peculiar bold and manly turn of thought. For our particular friends the Peripatetics, notwithstanding all their erudition, gravity, and flow of words, do not satisfy me about the moderation of these disorders and diseases of the soul, for every evil, though moderate, is in it nature great. But our business is to divest our wise man of all evil; for as the body is not sound, though but slightly affected, so the mind under any moderate disorder loses its soundness: therefore the Romans have with their usual skill called trouble, anguish, vexation, on account of the analogy between a troubled mind and a diseased body, disorders. The Greeks call all perturbation of mind by pretty nearly the same name, for they name every turbid motion of the soul *Παθος*, i. e. a distemper. But we have given them a more proper name; for a disorder of mind is very like a disease of the body. But lust doth not resemble sickness; neither doth immoderate joy, which is a high and exulting pleasure of the mind. Fear, too, is not very like a distemper, though it borders upon grief of mind, but properly as sickness of the body, it is so called from its connexion with pain; the same may be said of this grief: therefore I must explain whence this pain proceeds, i. e. the cause that occasions this grief, as it were a sickness of the body. For as physicians think they have found out the cure, when they have discovered the cause of the distemper, so we shall discover the method of cure when the cause is found out.

XI. The whole cause then is in opinion, not indeed of this grief alone, but of every other disorder of the mind; which are of four sorts, but consisting of many parts. For as every disorder or perturbation is a motion of the mind, either devoid of reason, or in despite of reason, or in disobedience to reason, and that motion is incited by an opinion of good and evil; these four perturbations are divided equally into two parts: for two of them proceed from an opinion of good; one of which is an exulting pleasure, i. e. a joy elate beyond measure, arising from an opinion of some present great good: the other, which may be rightly called either a desire or a lust, is an immoderate inclination after some conceived great good, in disobedience to reason. Therefore these two kinds, the exulting pleasure, and the lust, have their rise from an opinion of good, as the other two, fear and grief, from that of evil. For fear is an opinion of some great evil hanging over us; and grief is an opinion of some great evil present; and indeed it is a fresh conceived opinion of such an evil, that to grieve at it seems right. It is of that kind, that he who is uneasy at it thinks he has good reason to be so. Now we should exert our utmost efforts to oppose these perturbations, which are, as it were, so many furies let loose upon us by folly, if we are desirous to pass the share of life that is allotted us with any ease or satisfaction. But of the others I shall speak elsewhere: our business at present is to drive away grief if we can, for that is what I proposed; as you said it was your opinion a wise man might be subject to grief, which I can by no means allow of; for it is a frightful, horrid, and detestable thing, which we should fly from with our utmost efforts, with wind and tide, as I may say.

XII. That descendant of Tantalus, how doth he appear to you? He who sprung from Pelops, who formerly stole Hippodamia from her father-in-law, king Œnomaus, and married her by force? He who was descended from Jupiter himself,—how broken-hearted doth he seem!

> Stand off, my friends, nor come within my shade,
> That no pollutions your sound hearts pervade,
> So foul a stain my body doth partake.

Will you condemn yourself, Thyestes, and deprive yourself of life, on account of the greatness of another's crime? What! do you not look upon the son of the god of light, as unworthy his father's shining on him?

Hollow his eyes, his body worn away,
His furrow'd cheeks his frequent tears betray;
His beard neglected, his combined hairs,
Rough and uncomb'd, bespeak his bitter cares.

O foolish Œta, these are evils which you yourself are the cause of, and not occasioned by the accidents that befell you; and that you should behave thus, even when you had been inured to your distress, and after the first swelling of the mind had subsided! whereas grief consists (as I shall shew) in the notion of some recent evil: but your grief, I warrant you, proceeded from the loss of your kingdom, not your daughter; for you hated her, and perhaps with reason, but you could not calmly bear to part with your kingdom. But surely it is an impudent grief which preys upon a man for not being able to command those that are free. Dionysius, it is true, the tyrant of Syracuse, when driven from his country taught a school at Corinth; so incapable was he of living without some authority. What could be more impudent than Tarquin's making war against those who could not bear his tyranny; who, when he could not recover his kingdom by the forces of the Veientes and the Latins, is said to have betaken himself to Cuma, and to have died in that city, of old age and grief?

XIII. Do you then think it can befall a wise man to be oppressed with grief, i. e. with misery? for, as all perturbation is misery, grief is the rack itself; lust is attended with heat; exulting joy with levity; fear with a meanness; but grief with something greater than these; it consumes, torments, afflicts, and disgraces a man; it tears him, preys upon him, and quite puts an end to him. If we do not divest ourselves so of it, as to throw it quite off, we cannot be free from misery. And it is clear that there must be grief, where any thing has the appearance of a present sore and oppressing evil.

Epicurus is of opinion, that grief arises naturally from the imagination of any evil; that whosoever is eye-witness of any great misfortune, immediately conceives the like may befall himself, and becomes sad instantly on it. The Cyrenaics think, that grief doth not arise from every kind of evil, but from unexpected, unforeseen evil, and that is indeed of no small power to the heightening grief; for whatsoever comes of a sudden, is harder to bear. Hence these lines are deservedly commended:

> I knew my son, when first he drew his breath,
> Destin'd by fate to an untimely death;
> And when I sent him to defend the Greeks,
> Blows were his errand, not your sportive freaks.

XIV. Therefore this ruminating beforehand upon evils which you see at distance, makes their approach more tolerable; and on this account, what Euripides makes Theseus say, is much commended. You will give me leave to translate them into Latin, as is usual with me.

> I treasur'd up what some learn'd sage did tell,
> And on my future misery did dwell;
> I thought of bitter death, of being drove
> Far from my home by exile, and I strove
> With every evil to possess my mind,
> That, when they came, I the less care might find.

But Euripides speaks that of himself, which Theseus said he had heard from some learned man, for he was a hearer of Anaxagoras: who, as they relate, on hearing of the death of his son, said, "I knew my son was mortal;" which speech seems to intimate that such things afflict those who have not thought on them before. Therefore there is no doubt but that all evils are the heavier from not being foreseen. Though, notwithstanding that this circumstance alone doth not occasion the greatest grief; yet as the mind, by foreseeing and preparing for it, makes all grief the less, a man should consider all that may befall him in this life; and certainly the excellence of wisdom consists in taking a near view of things, and gaining a thorough experience in all human affairs; in not being surprised when any thing happens; and in thinking, before the event of things, that there is nothing but what may come to pass. Wherefore, at the very time that our affairs are in the best situation, at that very moment we should be most thoughtful how to bear a change of fortune. A traveller, at his return home, ought to be aware of such things as dangers, losses, &c. the debauchery of his son, the death of his wife, or a daughter's illness. He should consider that these are common accidents, and may happen to him, and should be no news to him if they do happen; but if things fall out better than he expected, he may look upon it as clear gain.

XV. Therefore, as Terence has so well expressed what he borrowed from philosophy, shall not we, the fountain from whence he drew it, say the same in a better manner, and abide by it more steadily? Hence is that same steady countenance, which, according to Xantippe, her husband Socrates always had: she never observed any difference in his looks when he went out, and when he came home. Yet the look of that old Roman M. Crassus, who, as Lucilius saith, never smiled but once in his lifetime, was not of this kind, but placid and serene, for so we are told. He indeed might well have the same look who never changed his mind, from whence the countenance has its expression. So that I am ready to borrow of the Cyrenaics those arms against the accidents and events of life, by means of which, by long premeditation, they break the force of all approaching evils; and at the same time, I think that those very evils themselves arise more from opinion than nature; for if they were real, no forecast could make them lighter. But I shall speak more particularly to these when I shall have first considered Epicurus's opinion, who thinks that all must necessarily be uneasy who perceive themselves in any evils, let them be either foreseen and expected, or habitual to them; for, with him, evils are not the less by reason of their continuance, nor the lighter for having been foreseen; and it is folly to ruminate on evils to come, or that, perhaps, may never come; every evil is disagreeable enough when it doth come: but he who is constantly considering that some evil may befall him, charges himself with a perpetual evil; for should such evil never light on him, he voluntarily takes to himself unnecessary misery, so that he is under constant uneasiness, whether he meets with any evil, or only thinks of it. But he places the alleviation of grief on two things, an avocation from thinking on evil, and a call to the contemplation of pleasure. For he thinks the mind may be under the power of reason, and follow her directions: he forbids us then to mind trouble, and calls us off from sorrowful reflections; he throws a mist over the contemplation of misery. Having sounded a retreat from these, he drives our thoughts on, and encourages them to view and engage the whole mind in the various pleasures, with which he thinks the life of a wise man abounds, either from reflecting on the past, or the hope of what is to come. I have said these things in my own way, the Epicureans have theirs; what they say is our business, how they say it is of little consequence.

XVI. In the first place, they are wrong in forbidding men to premeditate on futurity, for there is nothing that breaks the edge of grief and lightens it more, than considering, all life long, that there is nothing but what may happen; than considering what human nature is, on what conditions life was given, and how we may comply with them. The effect of which is, not to be always grieving, but never; for whoever reflects on the nature of things, the various turns of life, the weakness of human nature, grieves indeed at that reflection; but that grief becomes him as a wise man; for he gains these two points by it; when he is considering the state of human nature, he is enjoying all the advantage of philosophy, and is provided with a triple medicine against adversity. The first is, that he has long reflected that such things might befall him, which reflection alone contributes much towards lessening all misfortunes: the next is, that he is persuaded, that we should submit to the condition of human nature: the last is, that he discovers what is blameable to be the only evil. But it is not your fault that something lights on you, which it was impossible for man to avoid; for that withdrawing of our thoughts he recommends, when he calls us off from contemplating on our misfortunes, is imaginary; for it is not in our power to dissemble or forget those evils that lie heavy on us; they tear, vex, and sting us, they burn us up, and leave no breathing-time; and do you order us to forget them, which is against nature, and at the same time deprive us of the only assistance nature affords, the being accustomed to them, which, though it is a slow cure that time brings, is a very powerful one? You order me to employ my thoughts on something good, and forget my misfortunes. You would say something, and worthy a great philosopher, if you thought those things good which are best suited to the dignity of human nature.

XVII. Should Pythagoras, Socrates, or Plato, say to

me, why are you dejected, or grieve? Why do you faint, and yield to fortune, who perhaps may have power to harass and disturb you, but should not quite unman you? Virtue has great force, rouse your virtues if they droop. Take fortitude for your guide, which will give you such spirits, that you will despise every thing that can befall man, and look on them as trifles. Join to this temperance, which is moderation, and which was just now called frugality, which will not suffer you to do any thing base or bad; for what is worse or baser than an effeminate man? Not even justice will suffer you to do so, which seems to have the least weight in this affair, which notwithstanding will inform you that you are doubly unjust: when you require what doth not belong to you, that you who are born mortal, should be in the condition of the immortals, and take it much to heart that you are to restore what was lent you. What answer will you make to prudence, who acquaints you that she is a virtue sufficient of herself, both for a good life and a happy one? whom, it would be unreasonable to commend and so much desire, unless she were independent, having every thing centring in herself, and not obliged to look out for any supply, being self-sufficient. Now, Epicurus, if you invite me to such goods as these, I will obey, follow, and attend you as my guide, and even forget, as you order me, my misfortunes; and I do this much more readily from a persuasion that they are not to be ranked amongst evils. But you are for bringing my thoughts over to pleasure. What pleasures? pleasures of the body, I imagine, or such as are recollected or presumed on account of the body. Is this all? Do I explain your opinion right? for his disciples used to deny that we understand Epicurus. This is what he saith, and what that curious fellow old Zeno, who is one of the sharpest of them, used in my hearing at Athens to enforce and talk so loudly of; that he alone was happy, who could enjoy present pleasure, and who was persuaded that he should enjoy it without pain, either all or the greatest part of his life; or should any pain interfere, if it was the sharpest, it must be short; should it be of longer continuance, it would have more of sweet than bitter in it: that whosoever reflected on these things would be happy, especially if satisfied with the good things he had enjoyed, without fear of death, or the gods.

XVIII. You have here a representation of a happy life according to Epicurus, in the words of Zeno, so that there is no room for contradiction. What then? Can the proposing and thinking of such a life make Thyestes' grief the less, or Œta's, of whom I spoke above, or that of Telamon, who was driven from his country to penury and banishment? on whom they exclaimed thus:

Is this the man surpassing glory rais'd?
Is this that Telamon so highly prais'd
By wondering Greece, at whose sight, like the sun,
All others with diminish'd lustre shone?

Now, should any one like him be depressed with the loss of his fortune, he must apply to those old grave philosophers for relief, not to these voluptuaries: for what great good do they promise? Allow we, that to be without pain is the chief good? yet that is not called pleasure. But it is not necessary at present to go through the whole: the question is, if by advancing thus far we shall abate our grief? Grant that to be in pain is the greatest evil; whosoever then has proceeded so far as not to be in pain, is he therefore in immediate possession of the greatest good? What, Epicurus, do we use any evasions, and not allow in our own words the same to be pleasure, which you are used to boast of with such assurance? Are these your words or not? This is what you say in that book which contains all the doctrine of your school. I will perform the office of an interpreter, lest any should imagine I have invented. Thus you speak: "Nor can I form any notion of the chief good, abstracted from those pleasures which are perceived by taste, or from what depends on hearing music, or abstracted from ideas raised by external objects, which are agreeable motions; or those other pleasures, which are perceived by the whole man from his senses; nor can the pleasures of the mind be any ways said to constitute the only good: for I always perceived my mind to be pleased with the hopes of enjoying those things I mentioned above, and presuming I should enjoy them without any interruption from pain:" and from these words any one may understand what pleasure Epicurus was acquainted with. Then he speaks thus, a little lower down; "I have often inquired of those who are reputed to be wise men what would be the remaining good, if they should withdraw these, unless they meant to give us nothing but words? I could never learn any thing from them; and unless they choose that all virtue and wisdom should vanish and come to nothing, they must say with me, that the only road lies in those pleasures which I mentioned above." What follows is much the same, and his whole book on the chief good every where abounds with the same opinions. Will you then invite Telamon to this kind of life to ease his grief? and should you observe any of your friends under affliction, would you prescribe to him a sturgeon before a treatise of Socrates? or a concert rather than Plato? or lay before him the beauty and variety of some garden, present him with a nosegay, burn perfumes, and bid him be crowned with a garland of roses and woodbines? Should you add one thing more, you would certainly wipe out all his grief.

XIX. Epicurus must allow of these; or he must take out of his book what I just now said was a literal translation; or rather he must destroy his whole book, for it is stuffed with pleasures. We must inquire, then, how we can ease him of his grief, who can say thus:

My present state proceeds from fortune's stings;
My birth I boast of a descent from kings;
Hence may you see from what a noble height
I'm sunk by fortune to this abject plight.

What! to ease this grief, must we mix him a cup of sweet wine, or something of that kind? Lo! the same poet presents us with another somewhere else:

I, Hector, once so great, now claim your aid.

We should assist her, for she looks out for help:

Where shall I now apply, where seek support?
Where hence betake me, or to whom resort?
No means remain of comfort or of joy,
In flames my palace, and in ruins Troy;
Each wall, so late superb, deformed nods,
And not an altar left t' appease the gods.

You know what should follow, and particularly this:

Of father, country, and of friends bereft,
Not one of all those sumptuous temples left;
Which, whilst the fortune of our house did stand,
With rich wrought ceilings spoke the artist's hand.

O excellent poet! though despised by those who sing the verses of Euphorion. He is sensible that all things which come on a sudden are harder to be borne. Therefore, when he had set off the riches of Priam to the best advantage, which had the appearance of a long continuance, what doth he add?

Lo, these all perish'd in one blazing pile;
The foe old Priam of his life beguiled,
And with his blood thy altar, Jove, defiled.

Admirable poetry! There is something mournful in the subject, as well as the words and measure. We must drive away this grief of hers: how is that to be done? Shall we lay her on a bed of down; introduce a singer; shall we burn cedar, or present her with some pleasant liquor, and provide her something to eat? Are these the good things which remove the most afflicting grief? for you but just now said you knew of no other good. I should agree with Epicurus that we ought to be called off from grief to contemplate good things, were it once settled what was good.

XX. It may be said, What! do you imagine Epicurus really meant these, and that he maintained any thing so sensual? Indeed I do not imagine so, for I am sensible he has said many excellent things, and with great gravity. Therefore, as I said before, I am speaking of his acuteness, not his morals. Though he should hold those pleasures in contempt, which he just now commended, yet I must remember wherein he places the chief good. He did not barely say this, but he has explained what he would say: he saith, that taste, embracings, sports, and music, and those forms which affect the eyes with pleasure, are the chief good. Have I invented this? have I misrepresented him? I should be glad to be confuted; for what am I endeavouring at, but to clear up truth in every question? Well, but the same saith, that pleasure is at its height where pain ceases, and that to be free from all pain is the greatest pleasure. Here are three very great mistakes in a very few words. One is, that he contradicts himself; for, but just now, he could not imagine any thing good, unless the senses were in a manner tickled with some pleasure; but now, to be free from pain is the highest pleasure. Can any one contradict himself more? The other mistake is, that where there is naturally a threefold division, the first, to be pleased; next, not to be in pain; the last, to be equally distant from pleasure and pain: he imagines the first and the last to be the same, and makes no difference betwixt pleasure and a cessation of pain. The last mistake is in common with some others; which is this, that as virtue is the most desirable thing, and as philosophy was investigated for the attainment of it, he has separated the chief good from virtue: but he commends virtue, and that frequently; but indeed C. Gracchus, when he had made the largest distributions of the public money, and had exhausted the treasury, yet spoke much of preserving it. What signifies what they say, when we see what they do? That Piso who was surnamed Frugal, harangued always against the law that was proposed for distributing the corn, but when it had passed, though a consular man, he came to receive the corn. Gracchus observed Piso standing in the court, and asked him, in the hearing of the people, how it was consistent for him to take corn by a law he had himself opposed? "I was against your dividing my goods to every man as you thought proper, but, as you do so, I claim my share." Did not this grave and wise man sufficiently shew that the public revenue was dissipated by the Sempronian law? Read Gracchus's speeches, and you will pronounce him patron of the treasury. Epicurus denies that any one can live pleasantly who doth not lead a life of virtue; he denies that fortune has any power over a wise man: he prefers a spare diet to great plenty; maintains a wise man to be always happy:—all these things become a philosopher to say, but they are not consistent with pleasure. But the reply is, that he doth not mean *that* pleasure; let him mean any pleasure, it must be such a one as makes no part of virtue. But suppose we are mistaken as to his pleasure, are we so too as to pain? I maintain therefore the impropriety of that man's talking of virtue, who would measure every great evil by pain.

XXI. And indeed the Epicureans, those best of men, for there is no order of men more innocent, complain, that I take great pains to inveigh against Epicurus, as if we were rivals for some honour or distinction. I place the chief good in the mind, he in the body; I in virtue, he in pleasure: and the Epicureans are up in arms, and implore the assistance of their neighbours, and many are ready to fly to their aid. But, as for my part, I declare I am very indifferent about the matter, let it take what turn it may. For what! is the contention about the Punic war? on which very subject, though M. Cato and L. Lentulus were of different opinions, there was no difference betwixt them. These behave with too much heat, especially as the cause they would defend is no very reputable one, and for which they dare not plead either in the senate, or assembly of the people, before the army of the censors: but I will dispute this with them another time, and with such temper that no difference may arise, for I shall be ready to yield to their opinions when founded on truth. Only I must give them this advice; That were it ever so true, that a wise man regards nothing but the body; or, to express myself with more decency, has no view but to please himself, or to make all things depend on his own advantage; as such things are not very commendable, they should confine them to their own breasts, and leave off to talk with that parade of them.

XXII. What remains is the opinion of the Cyrenaics, who think that men grieve when any thing happens unexpectedly. And that is, indeed, as I said before, a great aggravation; and I know that it appeared so to Chrysippus, "Whatever falls out unexpected is so much the heavier." But the whole does not turn on this; though the sudden approach of an enemy sometimes occasions more confusion than when you expected him, and a sudden storm at sea throws the sailors into a greater fright than when they foresaw it, and it is the same in many cases. But when you carefully consider the nature of what was expected, you will find nothing more, than that all things which come on a sudden appear greater; and this upon two accounts. The first is, that you have not time to consider how great the accident is; the next is, when you are persuaded you could have guarded against them had you foreseen them, the misfortune seemingly contracted by your own fault makes your grief the greater. That it is so, time evinces; which as it advances, brings with it so much ease, that though the same misfortunes continue, the grief not only becomes the less, but in some cases is entirely removed. Many Carthaginians were slaves at Rome, many Macedonians when Perseus their king was taken prisoner. I saw, too, when I was a young man, some Corinthians in the Peloponnesus. They might all have lamented with Andromache,

All these I saw——.

But they had perhaps given over lamenting themselves, for by their countenances, speech, and other gestures, you might have taken them for Argives or Sicyonians. And I myself was more concerned at the ruined walls of Corinth, than the Corinthians themselves were, whose minds by frequent reflection and time had acquired a callousness. I have read a book of Clitomachus, which he sent to his captive citizens, to comfort them on the ruin of Carthage; there is in it a disputation written by Carneades, which, as Clitomachus saith, he had inserted into his commentary; the subject was, "Whether a wise man should seem to grieve at the captivity of his country?" You have there what Carneades said against it. There the philosopher applies such a strong medicine to a fresh grief, as would be quite unnecessary in one of any continuance; nor, had this very book been sent to the captives some years after, would it have found any wounds to cure, but scars; for grief, by a gentle progress and slow degrees, wears away imperceptibly. Not that the nature of things is altered, or can be, but that custom teaches what reason should, that those things lose their weight which before seemed to be of some consequence.

XXIII. It may be said, What occasion is there to apply to reason, or any consolation that we generally make use of, to ease the grief of the afflicted? For we have this always at hand, that there is nothing but what we may expect. But how will any one be enabled to bear his misfortunes the better by knowing that they are unavoidable? Saying thus subtracts nothing from the sum of the grief: it infers only that nothing has fallen out but what might have been thought of; and yet this manner of speaking has some little consolation in it, but, I apprehend, not much. Therefore those unlooked-for things have not so much force as to give rise to all our grief; the blow perhaps may fall the heavier, but whatever falls out doth not appear the greater on that account; no, it is because it has lately happened, not because it has befallen us unexpected, that makes it seem the greater. There are two ways then of discerning the truth, not only of things that seem evil, but of those that have the appearance of good. For we either inquire into the nature of the thing, what, and how great it is, as sometimes with regard to poverty; the burden of which we may lighten when by our disputations we shew how very little, how few things nature requires; or without any subtle arguing we refer them to examples, as here we instance in a Socrates, there in a Diogenes, and then again that line in Cæcilius,

Wisdom is oft conceal'd in mean attire.

For as poverty is of equal weight with all, what reason can be given, why what was borne by Fabricius should be insupportable by others? Of a piece with this is that other way of comforting, that nothing happens but what is common to human nature: now this argument doth not only inform us what human nature is, but implies that all things are tolerable which others have borne and can bear.

XXIV. Is poverty the subject? they tell you of many who have submitted to it with patience. Is it the contempt of honours? they acquaint you with some who never enjoyed any, and were the happier for it; and of those who have preferred a private retired life to public employment, mentioning their names with respect: they tell you of the verse of that most powerful king, who praises an old man, and pronounces him happy, who could reach old age in obscurity and without notice. Thus too they have examples for those who are deprived of their children; they who are under any great grief are comforted by instances of like affliction: thus every misfortune becomes the less by others having undergone the same. Reflection thus discovers to us how much opinion had imposed on us. And this is what that Telamon declares, "I knew my son was mortal;" and thus Theseus, "I on my future misery did dwell;" and Anaxagoras, "I knew my son was mortal." All these, by frequently reflecting on human affairs, discovered that they were by no means to be estimated by vulgar opinions: and indeed it seems to me to be pretty much the same with those who consider beforehand as with those who have their remedy from time, excepting that a kind of reason cures the one, the other is provided with this by nature; discovering thereby, that what was imagined to be the greatest evil, is not so great as to defeat the happiness of life. Thus it comes about, that the hurt which was not foreseen is greater, and not, as they suppose, that when the like misfortunes befall two different people, he only of them is affected with grief on whom it lights unexpectedly. So that some, under the oppression of grief, are said to have borne it worse on hearing of this common condition of man, that we are born under such conditions as render it impossible for a man to be exempt from all evil.

XXV. For this reason Carneades, as I see it in our Antiochus, used to blame Chrysippus for commending these verses of Euripides:

> Man, doom'd to care, to pain, disease, and strife,
> Walks his short journey thro' the vale of life:
> Watchful attends the cradle and the grave,
> And passing generations longs to save:
> Last dies himself: yet wherefore should we mourn?
> For man must to his kindred dust return;
> Submit to the destroying hand of fate,
> As ripen'd ears the harvest-sickle wait.

He would not allow a speech of this kind to avail at all to the cure of our grief, for he said it was a lamentable case itself, that we were fallen into the hands of such a cruel fate; for to preach up comfort from the misfortunes of another, is a comfort only to those of a malevolent disposition. But to me it appears far otherwise: for the necessity of bearing what is the common condition of humanity, makes you submit to the gods, and informs you that you are a man, which reflection greatly alleviates grief: and they do not produce these examples to please those of a malevolent disposition, but that any one in affliction may be induced to bear what he observes many others bear with tranquillity and moderation. For they who are falling to pieces, and cannot hold together through the greatness of their grief, should be supported by all kinds of assistance. From whence Chrysippus thinks that grief is called λυπην, as it were λυσις, i. e. a dissolution of the whole man. The whole of which I think may be pulled up by the roots, by explaining, as I said at the beginning, the cause of grief; for it is nothing else but an opinion and estimation of a present acute evil. Thus any bodily pain, let it be ever so grievous, may be tolerable where any hopes are proposed of some considerable good; and we receive such consolation from a virtuous and illustrious life, that they who lead such lives are seldom attacked by grief, or but slightly affected by it.

XXVI. But if to the opinion of evil there be added this other, that we ought to lament, that it is right so to do, and part of our duty; then is brought about that grievous disorder of mind. To which opinion we owe all those various and horrid kinds of lamentations, that neglect of our persons, that womanish tearing of our cheeks, that striking on our thighs, breasts, and heads. Thus Agamemnon, in Homer and in Accius,

Tears in his grief his uncomb'd locks.

From whence comes that pleasant saying of Bion, that the foolish king in his sorrow tore away the hairs of his head, imagining that being bald he would be less sensible of grief. But whoever acts thus is persuaded he ought to do so. And thus Æschines accuses Demosthenes of sacrificing within seven days after the death of his daughter. But how rhetorically! how copiously! what sentences has he collected? what words doth he throw out? You may see by this that an orator may do any thing, which nobody would have approved of, but from a prevailing opinion, that every good man ought to lament heavily the loss of a relation. Hence it comes, that some, when in sorrow, betake themselves to deserts; as Homer saith of Bellerophon,

> Wide o'er the Ælean field he chose to stray,
> A long, forlorn, uncomfortable way!
> Woes heap'd on woes consum'd his wasted heart;
>
> Pope, Il. b. vi. l. 247.

and thus Niobe is feigned to have been turned into stone, from her never speaking, I suppose, in her grief. But they imagine Hecuba to have been converted into a bitch, from her rage and bitterness of mind. There are others who love to converse with solitude itself, when in grief, as the nurse in Ennius,

> Fain would I to the heavens and earth relate
> Medea's ceaseless woes and cruel fate.

XXVII. Now all these things are done in grief, from a persuasion of the truth, rectitude, and necessity of them; and it is plain, that it proceeds from a conviction of its being their duty; for should these mourners by chance drop their grief, and seem more calm or cheerful for a moment, they presently check themselves and return to their lamentations again, and blame themselves for having been guilty of any intermissions from their grief. Parents and masters generally correct children not by words only, but by blows, if they shew any levity when the family is under affliction; and, as it were, oblige them to be sorrowful. What? doth it not appear, when you cease of course to mourn, and perceive your grief has been ineffectual, that the whole was an act of your own choosing? What saith he, in Terence, who punishes himself, i. e. the self-tormentor, "I am persuaded I do less injury to my son by being miserable myself." He determines to be miserable;

and can any one determine on any thing against his will? "I should think I deserved any misfortune." He should think he deserved any misfortune, were he otherwise than miserable. Therefore you see the evil is in opinion, not in nature. How is it, when some things prevent of themselves your grieving at them? as in Homer, so many died and were buried daily, that they had no leisure to grieve. Where you find these lines:

> The great, the bold, by thousands daily fall,
> And endless were the grief to weep for all.
> Eternal sorrows what avails to shed?
> Greece honours not with solemn fasts the dead:
> Enough when death demands the brave to pay
> The tribute of a melancholy day.
> One chief with patience to the grave resign'd,
> Our care devolves on others left behind.

Therefore it is in our own power to lay aside grief upon occasion; and is there any occasion (seeing the thing is in our own power) that we should let slip in order to get rid of care and grief? It was plain, that Cn. Pompey's friends, when they saw him fainting under his wounds, though at that very time they were under great uneasiness how they themselves, surrounded by the enemy, might escape, were employed in nothing but encouraging the rowers and aiding their escape; but when they reached Tyre, they began to grieve and lament over him. Therefore, as fear with them prevailed over grief, cannot reason and true philosophy have the same effect with a wise man?

XXVIII. But what is there more effectual to dispel grief than the discovery that it answers no purpose, and turns to no account? Therefore if we can get rid of it, we need never to have been subject to it. It must be acknowledged then that men take up grief wilfully and knowingly; and this appears from the patience of those who, after they have been exercised in afflictions and are better able to bear whatever befalls them, suppose themselves hardened against fortune, as that person in Euripides :

> Had this the first essay of fortune been,
> And I no storms thro' all my life had seen,
> Wild as a colt I'd broke from reason's sway,
> But frequent griefs have taught me to obey.

As then the frequent bearing of misery makes grief the lighter, we must necessarily perceive that the cause and original of it doth not lie in the thing itself. Your principal philosophers, or lovers of wisdom, though they have not yet arrived at it, are not they sensible that they are under the greatest evil? For they are fools, and folly is the greatest of all evils; and yet they lament not. How shall we account for this? Because that opinion is not fixed to that kind of evil: it is not our opinion, that it is right, meet, and our duty to be uneasy because we are not all wise men. Whereas this opinion is strongly affixed to that uneasiness where mourning is concerned, which is the greatest of all grief. Therefore Aristotle, when he blames some ancient philosophers for imagining that by their genius they had brought philosophy to the highest perfection, says, they must be either extremely foolish, or extremely vain; but that he himself could see that great improvements had been made therein in a few years, and that philosophy would in a little time arrive at perfection. Theophrastus is reported to have accused nature at his death for giving to stags and crows so long a life, which was of no use to them, and for giving so few days to men, where it would have been of the greatest use; whose days, had they been lengthened, the life of man would have been provided with all kinds of learning, and with arts in the greatest perfection. He lamented therefore that he should die just as he had begun to discover these. What? doth not every grave and distinguished philosopher acknowledge himself ignorant of many things? and that there are many things he must learn over and over again? and yet, though these are sensible that they stick in the very midway of folly, than which nothing can be worse, are under no great affliction, because the opinion that it is their duty to lament never interferes. What shall we say of those who think it unbecoming in a man to grieve? amongst whom we may reckon Q. Maximus, who buried his son that had been consul, and L. Paulus, who lost two sons within a few days of one another. Of the same opinion was M. Cato, who lost his son just as he was designed for Prætor: and many others, which I have collected in my book of Consolation. Now what made these so easy, but their persuasion that grief and lamentation was not becoming in a man? Therefore, as some give themselves up to grief from an opinion that it is right so to do, they refrained themselves from an opinion that it was wrong: from whence we may infer, that grief is owing more to opinion than nature.

XXIX. It may be said, on the other side, Who is so mad as to grieve voluntarily? Pain proceeds from nature; which you must submit to, agreeably to what even your own Crantor teaches, this presses and gains upon you unavoidably. So that the very same Oileus, in Sophocles, who had before comforted Telamon on the death of Ajax, on hearing of the death of his own son is broken-hearted. On this alteration of his mind we have these lines:

> Shew me the man so well by wisdom taught
> That what he charges to another's fault,
> When like affliction doth himself betide,
> True to his own wise counsel will abide.

Now when they urge these, their endeavour is to evince, that nature is irresistible; and yet the same people allow, that we take greater grief on ourselves than nature requires. What madness is it then in us to require the same from others? But there are many reasons for taking grief on us. The first is from the opinion of some evil, on the discovery and persuasion of which, grief comes of course. Besides, many people are persuaded they do something very acceptable to the dead when they lament over them. To these may be added a kind of womanish superstition, in imagining that to acknowledge themselves afflicted and humbled by the gods, is the readiest way of appeasing them. But few see what contradictions these things are charged with. They commend those who die calmly, but they blame those who can bear the loss of another with the same calmness; as if it were possible that it should be true, as lovers say, that any one can love another more than himself. There is indeed something excellent in this, and, if you examine it, no less just than true, that we should love those who ought to be dear to us, as well as we love ourselves; but to love them more than ourselves is impossible; nor is it desirable in friendship that I should love my friend more than myself, or he me: this would occasion much confusion in life, and break in upon all the duties of it.

XXX. But of this elsewhere: at present it is sufficient not to lay our misery to the loss of our friends, nor to love them more than, were they sensible, they would approve of, or at least more than we do ourselves. Now as to what they say, that some are not all eased by our consolations; and moreover add, that the comforters themselves acknowledge they are miserable when fortune varies the attack and falls on them,—in both these cases the solution is easy: for the fault here is not in nature, but our own folly, and much may be said against folly. But not to admit of consolation seems to bespeak their own misery; and they who cannot bear their misfortunes with that temper they recommend to others, they are but on a footing with the covetous, who find fault with those that are so; as do the vain-glorious with those of the same turn with themselves. For it is the peculiar characteristic of folly to discover the vices of others, forgetting its own. But since we find that grief is removed by length of time, we have the greatest proof that the strength of it depends not merely on time, but the daily consideration of it. For if the cause continues the same, and the man be the same, how can there be any alteration in the grief, if there is no change in what occasioned the grief, nor in him who grieves? Therefore it is from daily reflecting that it is no evil for which you grieve, and not from the length of time, that you have the cure of grief.

XXXI. Here some talk of moderate grief, which, supposing it natural, what occasion is there for consolation? for nature herself will determine the measure of it; but if it is in opinion, the whole opinion may be destroyed. I think it has been sufficiently said, that grief arises from an opinion of some present evil which includes this, that it is incumbent on us to grieve. To this definition Zeno has added very justly, that the opinion of this present evil should be recent. Now this word recent is explained thus; not that alone is recent which happened a little while ago, but, as long as there shall be any force or vigour or freshness in that imagined evil, so long it is entitled to the name of recent. As Artemisia, the wife of Mausolus king of Caria, who made that noble sepulchre at Halicarnassus; whilst she lived she lived in grief, and died of that.

being worn out by it, so that that opinion was always recent with her: but you cannot call that so, which in time decays. Now the duty of a comforter is, to remove grief entirely, to quiet it, or draw it off as much as you can, to keep it under, and prevent its spreading, or to divert it. There are some who think with Cleanthes, that the only duty of a comforter is to prove, that it is by no means any evil. Others, as the Peripatetics, that the evil is not great. Others, with Epicurus, lead you off from the evil to good: some think it sufficient to shew, that nothing has happened but what you had reason to expect. But Chrysippus thinks the main thing in comforting is, to remove the opinion from the person who is grieving, that to grieve is his bounden duty. There are others who bring together all these various kinds of consolations, for people are differently affected; as I have done myself in my book of Consolation: for my own mind being much disordered, I have given in that every method of cure. But the proper season is as much to be watched in the cure of the mind, as of the body; as Prometheus in Æschylus, on its being said to him,

> I think, Prometheus, you this tenet hold,
> That all men's reason should their rage control;

answers,

> Yes, when one reason properly applies;
> Ill-tim'd advice will make the storm but rise.

XXXII. But the principal medicine to be applied in consolation, is to maintain either that it is no evil at all, or a very inconsiderable one: next to that is, to speak to the common condition of life, and with a view, if possible, to the state of the person whom you comfort particularly. The third is, that it is folly to wear oneself out with grief which can avail nothing. For the advice of

Cleanthes is for a wise man who wants none; for could you persuade one in grief, that nothing is an evil but what is base, you would not only cure him of grief, but folly. But the time for such doctrine is not well chosen. Besides, Cleanthes doth not seem to me sufficiently apprised, that affliction may very often proceed from that very thing which he himself allows to be the greatest misfortune. As was the case with Alcibiades, whom Socrates convinced, as we are told, that there was no difference betwixt him, though a man of the first fashion, and a porter. Alcibiades, being uneasy at this, entreated Socrates with tears in his eyes, to make him a man of virtue, and dismiss that baseness. What shall we say to this, Cleanthes? Was there no evil in what afflicted Alcibiades thus? What strange things doth Lycon say? who, to assuage grief, makes it arise from trifles, from things that affect our fortune or bodies, not from the evils of the mind. What, then, did not the grief of Alcibiades proceed from the vices and evils of the mind? I have already said enough of Epicurus's consolation.

XXXIII. Nor is that consolation much to be relied on, though frequently practised, and sometimes having effect, viz. That you are not alone in this. It has its effect, as I said, but not always, nor with every person; for some reject it, but much depends on the application of it; for you are to set forth, not how men in general have been affected with evils, but how men of sense have borne them. As to Chrysippus's method, it is certainly founded in truth; but it is difficult to apply it in time of distress. It is a work of no small difficulty to persuade a person in affliction that he grieves, merely because he thinks it right so to do. Certainly then, as in pleadings we do not state all cases alike, but adjust them to the time, to the nature of the subject under debate, and the person; thus in assuaging grief, regard should be had to what kind of cure the party will admit of. But, I know not how, we have rambled from what you proposed. For your question was concerning a wise man, with whom nothing can have the appearance of evil, that is not dishonourable: or at least would seem so small an evil, that by his wisdom he so overmatches it, that it quite disappears; who makes no addition to his grief through opinion; who never conceives it right to torment himself above measure, and wear himself out with grief, which is the meanest thing imaginable. Reason, however, it seems, has evinced, though it was not directly our subject at present, that nothing can be called an evil but what is base; and, by the way, we may discover, that all the evil of affliction has nothing natural in it, but is contracted by our own voluntary judgment of it, and the error of opinion. Therefore I have treated of that kind of affliction, which is the greatest; the removing of which has made it of little consequence to look after remedies for others.

XXXIV. There are certain things usually said on poverty; others on a retired and undistinguished life. There are particular treatises on banishment, on the ruin of one's country, on slavery, on weakness or blindness, and on every incident that can come under the name of an evil. The Greeks divide these into different treatises and distinct books: but they do it for the sake of employment: not but that disputations are full of entertainment; and yet, as physicians, in curing the whole body, help the least part that is affected, so philosophy, after it has removed grief in general, if any other deficiency exist; should poverty bite, should ignominy sting, should banishment bring a dark cloud over us, or should any of those things I just mentioned appear, it applies to each its particular consolation: which you shall hear whenever you please. But we must have recourse to the same fountain, that a wise man is free from all evil, because it is insignificant, because it answers no purpose, because it is not founded in nature, but opinion and prejudice, but a kind of courting grief, when once they have imagined that it is their duty to do so. Subtracting then what is altogether voluntary, that mournful uneasiness will be removed; yet some little anxiety, some small remorse will remain. They may indeed call this natural, provided they give it not that horrid, solemn, melancholy name of grief, which can by no means consist with wisdom. But how various, and how bitter, are the roots of grief! Whatever they are, I propose, after having felled the trunk, to destroy them all; and if you approve of it, by particular dissertations, for I have leisure enough, whatever time it may take up. But it is the same with all uneasiness, though it appears under different names. For envy is an uneasiness; so are emulation, detraction, anguish, sorrow, sadness, tribulation, lamentation, vexation, grief, trouble, affliction, and despair. The Stoics define all these, and all those words I mentioned belong to different things, and do not, as they seem, express the same things; but they are distinct, as I shall make appear perhaps in another place. These are those fibres of the roots, which, as I said at first, must be cut off, and destroyed, that not one should remain. You say it is a great and difficult undertaking; who denies it? But what is there of any excellency which has not its difficulty? Yet philosophy undertakes to effect it, provided we accept of the cure. But so much for this: the others, whenever you please, shall be ready for you here, or any where else.

BOOK IV.

ON OTHER PERTURBATIONS OF THE MIND.

I HAVE been apt to wonder, Brutus, on many occasions, at the ingenuity and virtues of our countrymen; but nothing has surprised me more than those studies, which, though they came somewhat late to us, have been transported into this city from Greece. For the auspices, religious ceremonies, courts of justice, appeals to the people, the senate, the establishment of horse and foot, and the whole military discipline, were instituted as early as the foundation of the city by royal authority, partly too by laws, not without the assistance of the gods. Then with what a surprising and incredible progress did they advance towards all kind of excellence, when once the Republic was freed from the regal power? Not that I propose to treat here of the manners and customs of our ancestors, the discipline and constitution of the city; for I have elsewhere, particularly in the six books I wrote on the Republic, given a very accurate account of them. But whilst I am on this subject, and considering the study of philosophy, I meet with many reasons to imagine that those studies were brought to us from abroad, and not merely imported, but preserved and improved; for they had Pythagoras, a man of consummate wisdom, in a manner, before their eyes; who was in Italy at the time L. Brutus, the illustrious founder of your nobility, delivered his country from tyranny. As the doctrine of Pythagoras spread itself on all sides, it seems probable to me, that it reached this city: and this is not only probable, but appears to have been the case from many remains of it. For who can imagine, that, when it flourished so much in that part of Italy which was called Greece, in some of the largest and most powerful cities, in which, first, the name of Pythagoras, and then theirs, who were afterwards his followers, was in so high esteem; who can imagine, I say, that our people could shut their ears to what was said by such learned men? Besides, my opinion is, that the great esteem the Pythagoreans were held in, gave rise to that opinion amongst our ancestors, that king Numa was a Pythagorean. For, being acquainted with the discipline and institutes of Pythagoras, and having heard from their ancestors, that the king was a very wise and just man, and not being able to distinguish times that were so remote, they inferred, from his being so eminent for his wisdom, that he was a hearer of Pythagoras.

II. So far we proceed on conjecture. As to the vestiges of the Pythagoreans, though I might collect many, I shall use but a few; because that is not our present purpose. Now, as it is reported to have been a custom with them to deliver certain abstruse precepts in verse, and to bring their minds from severe thought to a more composed state by songs and musical instruments; so Cato, a very serious author, saith in his Origins, that it was customary with our ancestors for the guests at their entertainments, every one in his turn, to sing the praises and virtues of illustrious men to the sound of the flute: from whence it is clear that poems and songs were then composed for the voice. Still, that poetry was in fashion appears from the laws of the twelve tables, wherein it is provided, that none should be made to the injury of another. Another argument of the erudition of those times is, that they played on instruments before the feasts held in honour of their gods, and the entertainments of their magistrates: now that was peculiar to the sect I am speaking of. To me, indeed, that poem of Appius

Cæcus, which Panætius commends so much in a certain letter to Q. Tubero, has all the marks of a Pythagorean. We have many things derived from them in our customs: which I pass over, that we may not seem to have learned that elsewhere which we look on ourselves as the inventors of. But to return to our purpose. How many great poets as well as orators have sprung up among us! and in what a short time! so that it is evident, that our people could attain any thing as soon as they had an inclination for it. But of other studies I shall speak elsewhere if there is occasion, as I have already often done.

III. The study of philosophy is certainly of long standing with us; but yet I do not find that I can give you the names of any before the age of Lælius and Scipio: in whose younger days we find that Diogenes the Stoic, and Carneades the Academic, were sent ambassadors by the Athenians to our senate. As these had never been concerned in public affairs, and one of them was a Cyrenean, the other a Babylonian, they had certainly never been forced from their studies, nor chosen for that employ, unless the study of philosophy had been in vogue with some of the great men at that time: who, though they might employ their pens on other subjects; some on civil law, others on oratory, others on the history of former times, yet promoted this most extensive of all arts, the discipline of living well, more by their life than by their writings. So that of that true and elegant philosophy, (which was derived from Socrates, and is still preserved by the Peripatetics, and by the Stoics, though they express themselves differently in their disputes with the Academics,) there are few or no Latin monuments; whether this proceeds from the importance of the thing itself, or from men's being otherwise employed, or from their concluding that the capacity of the people was not equal to the apprehension of them. But, during this silence, C. Amafinius arose and took upon himself to speak; on the publishing of whose writings the people were moved, and enlisted themselves chiefly under this sect, either because the doctrine was more easily understood, or that they were invited thereto by the pleasing thoughts of amusement, or that, because there was nothing better, they laid hold of what was offered them. And after Amafinius, when many of the same sentiments had written much about them, the Pythagoreans spread over all Italy: but that these doctrines should be so easily understood and approved of by the unlearned, is a great proof that they were not written with any great subtlety, and they think their establishment to be owing to this.

IV. But let every one defend his own opinion, they are at liberty to choose what they like: I shall keep to my old custom; and being under no restraint from the laws of any particular school, which in philosophy every one must necessarily confine himself to, I shall always inquire after what has the most probability in every question, which, as I have often practised on other occasions, I have kept close to in my Tusculan Disputations. Therefore, as I have acquainted you with the disputations of the three former days, this book concludes the fourth. When we had come down into the academy, as we had done the former days, the business was carried on thus. *M.* Let any one say, who pleases, what he would have disputed. *A.* I do not think a wise man can possibly be free from every perturbation of mind. *M.* He seemed by yesterday's discourse to be so from grief: unless you allowed it only not to take up time. *A.* Not at all on that account, for I was extremely satisfied with your discourse. *M.* You do not think then that a wise man is subject to grief? *A.* No, by no means.

M. But if that cannot disorder the mind of a wise man, nothing else can. For what? can it be disturbed by fear? Fear proceeds from the same things when absent, which occasion grief when present. Take away grief then, and you remove fear.

V. The two remaining perturbations are, a joy elate above measure, and lust: which if a wise man is not subject to, his mind will be always at rest. *A.* I am entirely of that opinion. *M.* Had you rather, then, that I should immediately crowd all my sails? or shall I make use of my oars, as if I were just endeavouring to get clear of the harbour? *A.* I do not apprehend what you mean by that. *M.* Why, Chrysippus and the Stoics, when they dispute on the perturbations of the mind, make great part of their debate to consist in dividing and distinguishing: they employ but few words on the subject of curing the mind, and preventing it from being disordered. Whereas the Peripatetics bring a great many things to promote the cure of it, but have no regard to their thorny partitions and definitions. My question then was, whether I should instantly unfold the sails of my discourse, or make my way out with the oars of the logicians? *A.* Let it be so: for by means of both these, the subject of our inquiry will be more thoroughly discussed. *M.* It is certainly the better way: and should any thing be too obscure, you may inform yourself afterwards. *A.* I will do so; but those very obscure things, you will, as usual, deliver with more clearness than the Greeks. *A.* I will indeed endeavour to do so: but it requires great attention, for should you lose one word, the whole will escape you. What the Greeks call πάθη, we choose to name perturbations (or disorders) rather than diseases, in explaining which, I shall follow, first, that very old description of of Pythagoras, then Plato's; who divide the mind into two parts; they make one of these to partake of reason, the other to be without it. In that which partakes of reason they place tranquillity, i. e. a placid and undisturbed constancy: to the other they assign the turbid motions of anger and desire, which are contrary and opposite to reason. Let this then be our principle, the spring of all our reasonings. But notwithstanding, I shall use the partitions and definitions of the Stoics in describing these perturbations: who seem to me to have been very subtle on this question.

VI. Zeno's definition, then, is thus: that a perturbation, which he calls a πάθος, is a commotion of the mind repugnant to reason, and against nature. Some of them define it shorter; that a perturbation is a more vehement appetite; but by more vehement they mean an appetite that recedes further from the constancy of nature. But they would have the distinct parts of perturbations to arise from two imagined goods, and from two imagined evils: and thus they become four: from the good proceed lust and joy: as joy from some present good, lust from future. They suppose fear and grief to proceed from evils: fear from something future, grief from something present: for whatever things are dreaded as approaching, always occasion grief when present. But joy and lust depend on the opinion of good: as lust is inflamed and provoked, and carried eagerly to what has the appearance of good; joy is transported and exults on obtaining what was desired. For we naturally pursue those things that have the appearance of good; and fly the contrary. Wherefore, as soon as any thing that has the appearance of good presents itself, nature incites us to the obtaining it. Now where this is consistent and founded on prudence, this strong desire is by the Stoics called βούλησις, but we name it a volition; and this they allow to none but their wise man, and define it thus. Volition is a reasonable desire, but whatever is incited too violently in opposition to reason, that is a lust, or an unbridled desire; which is discoverable in all fools. And with respect to good, we are likewise moved two ways; there is a placid and calm motion, consistent with reason, called joy: and there is likewise a vain, wanton exultation, or immoderate joy, *lætitia gestiens*, or transport, which they define to be an elation of the mind without reason. And as we naturally desire good things, so in like manner we naturally avoid evil; the avoiding of which, if warranted by reason, is called caution; and this the wise man alone is supposed to have: but that caution which is not under the guidance of reason, but is attended with a base and low dejection, is called fear. Fear is therefore an unreasonable caution. A wise man is not affected by any present evil: but the grief of a fool proceeds from being affected with an imaginary evil, on which their minds are contracted and sunk, as they revolt from reason. This, then, is the first definition, which makes grief to consist in the mind's shrinking contrary to the dictates of reason. Thus there are four perturbations, and but three opposites, for grief has no opposite.

VII. But they would have all perturbations depend on opinion and judgment; therefore they define them more closely; not only the better to shew how blameable they are, but to discover how much they are in our power. Grief then is a recent opinion of some evil, in which it seems to be right, that the mind should shrink and be dejected. Joy, a recent opinion of a present good, in which it seems to be right that the mind should be transported. Fear, an opinion of an impending evil, which we apprehend as intolerable. Lust, an opinion of a good to come, which would be of advantage were it already come, and present with us. But however I have named the judgments and opinions of perturbations, their meaning is not that merely the perturbations consist in them; but the effects likewise of these perturbations: as grief occasions a kind of painful remorse; fear, a recoil or sudden escape of the mind; joy, a profuse mirth; lust, an unbridled habit of coveting. But that imagination, which I have included in all the above definitions, they would have to consist in assenting without warrantable grounds. Now every perturbation has many parts annexed to it of the same kind. Grief is attended with enviousness (I use that word for instruction sake, though it is not so common; because envy takes in not only the person who envies, but the person too who is envied). Emulation, detraction, pity, vexation, mourning, sadness, tribulation, sorrow, lamentation, solicitude, disquiet of mind, pain, despair, and whatever else, is of this kind. Fear includes sloth, shame, terror, cowardice, fainting, confusion, astonishment. In pleasure they comprehend a malevolence that is pleased at another's misfortune, a delight, boasting, and the like. To lust they associate anger, fury, hatred, enmity, discord, wants, desire, and the rest of that kind.

VIII. But they define these in this manner. Envying, they say, is a grief arising from the prosperous circumstances of another, which are no ways detrimental to the person who envies: for where any one grieves at the prosperity of another, by which he is injured, such an one is not properly said to envy; as when Agamemnon grieves at Hector's success: but where any one, who is no ways hurt by the prosperity of another, is in pain at his success, such an one envies indeed. Now that emulation is taken in a double sense, so that the same word may stand for praise and dispraise: for the imitation of virtue is called emulation; but that sense of it I shall have no occasion for here; for that carries praise with it. Emulation is also grief at another's enjoying what I desired to have, and am without. Detraction (and I mean by that, jealousy) is a grief even at another's enjoying what I had a great inclination for. Pity is a grief at the misery of another, who suffers wrongfully: no one grieves at the punishment of a parricide, or of a betrayer of his country. Vexation is a pressing grief. Mourning is a grief at the bitter death of one who was dear to you. Sadness is a grief attended with tears. Tribulation is a painful grief. Sorrow, an excruciating grief. Lamentation, a grief where we loudly bewail ourselves. Solicitude, a pensive grief. Trouble, a continued grief. Affliction, a grief that harasses the body. Despair, a grief that excludes all hope of better things to come. What is included under fear, they define to be sloth, which is a dread of some ensuing labour: shame and terror, that affects the body; hence blushing attends shame; a paleness and tremor, and chattering of the teeth, terror: cowardice, an apprehension of some approaching evil; dread, a fear that unhinges the mind, whence comes that of Ennius,

> Then dread discharg'd all wisdom from my mind:

fainting is the associate and constant attendant on dread; confusion, a fear that drives away all thought; astonishment, a continued fear.

IX. The parts they assign to pleasure come under this description, that malevolence is a pleasure in the misfortunes of another without any advantage to yourself: delight, a pleasure that soothes the mind by agreeable impressions on the ear. What is said of the ear, may be applied to the sight, to the touch, smell, and taste. All of this kind are a sort of melting pleasures that dissolve the mind. Boasting is a pleasure that consists in making an appearance, and setting off yourself with insolence. What comes under lust they define in this manner. Anger is a lust of punishing any one we imagine has injured us without cause. Heat is anger just forming and beginning to exist, which the Greeks call θύμωσις. Hatred is a settled anger. Enmity is anger waiting for an opportunity of revenge. Discord is a sharper anger conceived deep in the mind and heart. Want, an insatiable lust. Desire, is when one eagerly wishes to see a person who is absent. Now here they have a distinction: desire is a lust conceived on hearing of certain things reported of some one, or of many, which the Greeks call predicated; as that they are in possession of riches and honours: but want is a lust for those very honours and riches. But they make intemperance the fountain of all these perturbations: which is an absolute revolt from the mind and right reason: a state so averse to all prescriptions of reason, that the appetites of the mind are by no means to be governed and restrained. As therefore temperance appeases these desires, making them obey right reason, and maintains the well-weighed judgments of the mind; so intemperance, which is in opposition to this, inflames, confounds, and puts every state of the mind into a violent motion. Thus grief and fear, and every other perturbation of the mind, have their rise from intemperance.

X. Just as distempers and sickness are bred in the

body from the corruption of the blood, and the too great abundance of phlegm and bile; so the mind is deprived of its health, and disordered with sickness, from a confusion of depraved opinions, that are in opposition to one another. From these perturbations arise, first, diseases, which they call *νοσηματα;* in opposition to these are certain faulty distastes or loathings; then sicknesses, which are called *ἀῤῥωστηματα* by the Stoics; and these two have their opposite aversions. Here the Stoics, especially Chrysippus, give themselves unnecessary trouble to shew the analogy the diseases of the mind have with those of the body: but, overlooking all that they say as of little consequence, I shall treat only of the thing itself. Let us then understand perturbation to imply a restlessness from the variety and confusion of contradictory opinions; and that when this heat and disturbance of the mind is of any standing, and has taken up its residence, as it were, in the veins and marrow, then commence diseases and sickness, and those aversions which are in opposition to them.

XI. What I say here may be distinguished in thought, though they are in fact the same; and have their rise from lust and joy. For should money be the object of our desire, and should we not instantly apply to reason, Socrates' medicine to heal this desire, the evil slides into our veins, and cleaves to our bowels, and from thence proceeds a distemper or sickness, which, when of any continuance, is incurable. The name of this disease is covetousness. It is the same with other diseases; as the desire of glory, a passion for women, if I may so call *φιλογυνεια;* and thus all other diseases and sicknesses are generated. Now, the contrary of these are supposed to have fear for their foundation, as a hatred of women, such as is the Woman-hater of Atilius: or the hating the whole human species, as Timon is reported to have done, whom they called the Misanthrope. Of the same kind is inhospitality. All which diseases proceed from a certain dread of such things as they hate and avoid. But they define sickness of mind to be an overweening opinion, and that fixed and settled, of something as very desirable, which is by no means so. What proceeds from aversion, they define thus: a vehement conceit of something to be avoided, when there is no reason for avoiding it; and thus a fixed and settled conceit. Now this conceit is a persuasion that you know what you are ignorant of. But this sickness is attended with something like these; covetousness, ambition, a passion for women, wilfulness, gluttony, drunkenness, luxury, conceit, and the like. For covetousness is a vehement imagination of money, which strongly possesses you that it is a very desirable thing: and in like manner they define other things of the same kind. The definitions of aversions are after this sort; inhospitality is a vehement opinion, with which you are strongly possessed, that you should avoid a stranger. Thus too the hatred of women, like Hippolitus's, is defined, and the hatred of the human species, like Timon's.

XII. But to come to the analogy of the state of body and mind, which I shall sometimes make use of, though more sparingly than the Stoics: as some are more inclined to particular disorders than others. Thus we say, that some are rheumatic, others dropsical, not because they are so at present, but because they are often so: some are more inclined to fear, others to some other perturbation. Thus in some there is an anxiety, whence they are anxious; in some a hastiness of temper, which differs from anger, as anxiety differs from anguish: for all are not anxious who are sometimes vexed; nor are they who are anxious always uneasy in that manner: as there is a difference betwixt being drunk, and drunkenness; and it is one thing to be a lover, another to be given to women. And this disposition of some to particular disorders, is very extensive: for it relates to all perturbations; it appears in many vices, though it has no name: some are therefore said to be envious, malevolent, spiteful, fearful, pitiful, from a propensity to those perturbations, not from their being always carried away by them. Now this propensity to these particular disorders may be called a sickness, from analogy with the body; that is, nothing more than a propensity towards sickness. But with regard to whatever is good, as some are more inclined to different goods than others, we may call this a facility or tendency: this tendency to evil is a proclivity or inclination to falling: but where any thing is neither good, nor bad, it may have the former name.

XIII. Even as there may be, with respect to the body, a disease, a sickness, and a defect; so it is with the mind. They call that a disease where the whole body is corrupted: sickness, where a disease is attended with a weakness: a defect, where the parts of the body are not well compacted together; from whence it follows, that the members are mis-shaped, crooked, and deformed. So that these two, a disease and sickness, proceed from a violent concussion and perturbation of the health of the whole body; but a defect discovers itself, even when the body is in perfect health. But a disease of the mind is distinguishable only in thought from a sickness. A viciousness is a habit or affection discordant and inconsistent throughout life. Thus it happens, that a disease and sickness may arise from one kind of corruption of opinions; from another inconstancy and inconsistency.

For every vice of the mind doth not imply a disunion of parts; as is the case with those who are not far from wise men: with them there is that affection which is inconsistent with itself whilst it is witless, but it is not distorted, nor depraved. But diseases and sicknesses are parts of viciousness: but it is a question whether perturbations are parts of the same: for vices are permanent affections; perturbations are affections that are restless; so that they cannot be parts of permanent affections. As there is some analogy between the nature of the body and mind in evil, so in good: for the distinctions of the body are beauty, strength, health, firmness, quickness of motion; the same may be said of the mind. The body is said to be in a good state, when all those things on which health depends are consistent: the same may be said of the mind, when its judgments and opinions are not at variance. And this union is the virtue of the mind: which, according to some, is temperance itself; others make it consist in an obedience to the precepts of temperance, and a complying with them, not allowing it to be any distinct species of itself: but be it one or the other, it is to be found only in a wise man. But there is a certain soundness of mind, which a fool may have, when the perturbation of his mind is removed by the care and management of his physicians. And as what is called beauty arises from an exact proportion of the limbs, together with a sweetness of complexion, so the beauty of the mind consists in an equality and constancy of opinions and judgments, joined to a certain firmness and stability, pursuing virtue, or containing within itself the very essence of virtue. Besides, we give the very same names to the faculties of the mind, as we do to the powers of the body, the nerves, and other powers of action. Thus the velocity of the body is called swiftness: a praise we entitle the mind to, from its running over in its thoughts so many things in so short a time.

XIV. Herein indeed the mind and body are unlike: that though the mind when in perfect health may be visited by sickness, as the body may, yet the body may be disordered without our fault, the mind cannot. For all the disorders and perturbations of the mind proceed from a neglect of reason; these disorders therefore are confined to men; the beasts are not subject to perturbations, though they act sometimes as if they had reason. There is a difference, too, betwixt ingenious and dull men; the ingenious, like the Corinthian brass, which is long before it receives rust, are longer before they fall into these perturbations, and are recovered sooner; the case is different with the dull. Nor doth the mind of an ingenious man fall into every kind of perturbation, never into any that are brutish and savage: some of their perturbations have the appearance of humanity, as mercy, grief, and fear. The sicknesses and diseases of the mind are thought to be harder to pluck up, than those leading vices which are in opposition to virtues: for vices may be removed, though the diseases of the mind should continue, which diseases are not cured with that expedition vices are removed. I have now acquainted you with what the Stoics dispute with such exactness; which they call logic, from their close arguing: and since my discourse has got clear of these rocks, I will proceed with the remainder of it, provided I have been sufficiently clear in what I have already said, considering the obscurity of the subject I have treated. *A.* Clear enough; but should there be occasion for a more exact inquiry, I shall take another opportunity: I expect you to hoist your sail, as you just now called it, and proceed on your course.

XV. *M.* Since I have before said of virtue in other places, and shall often have occasion to say (for a great many questions that relate to life and manners arise from the spring of virtue); since, I say, virtue consists in a settled and uniform affection of mind, bringing praise to those who are possessed of her; she herself, independent of any thing else, without regard to any advantage, must be praiseworthy; for from her proceed good inclinations, opinions, actions, and the whole of right reason; though virtue may be defined in few words to be right reason itself. The opposite to this is viciousness, (for so I choose to define what the Greeks call *κακίαν*, rather than perverseness; for perverseness is the name of a particular vice; but viciousness includes all,) from whence arise those perturbations, which, as I just now said, are turbid and violent motions of the mind, repugnant to reason, and enemies in a high degree to the peace of the mind, and a tranquil life: for they introduce piercing cares, afflicting and debilitating the mind through fear; they violently inflame our appetites; occasioning that impotence of mind, utterly different from temperance and moderation, which I sometimes call desire, sometimes lust, which, should it attain its desires, becomes so elate, that it loses all its resolution, and knows not what to pursue; so that he was in the right who said, "that too great a joy was founded on a great mistake." Virtue then alone can effect the cure of these evils.

XVI. For what is not only more miserable, but more base and sordid, than a man afflicted, weakened, and oppressed with grief? Little short of this misery is one who dreads some approaching evil, and who, through faintheartedness, is under continual suspense. The poets, to express the greatness of this evil, imagine a stone to hang over the head of Tantalus, for his wickedness, his pride, and his boasting. Folly is punished generally in the same way; for there hangs over the head of every one who revolts from reason something of this kind, either grief or fear. And as these perturbations of the mind, grief and fear, are of a poisonous nature; so those two others, though of a more merry cast, (I mean lust, which is always coveting, and empty mirth, which is an exulting joy,) differ very little from madness. Hence you may understand what I mean by calling a man sometimes moderate, then modest or temperate, at another time constant and virtuous; sometimes I would include all these names in the word frugality, as the crown of all. For if that word did not include all virtues, it would never have been proverbial to say, that a frugal man doth every thing right; which, when the Stoics apply to their wise man, they seem to exalt him too much, and to speak of him with too much admiration.

XVII. Whoever then, through moderation and constancy, is at rest in his mind, and in calm possession of himself, so as neither to pine with care, nor be dejected with fear, neither to be inflamed with desire, nor dissolved by extravagant joy, such a one is the very wise man we inquire after, the happy man: to whom nothing in this life seems so intolerable as to depress him; nothing so exquisite as to transport him. For what is there in this life that can appear great to him, who has acquainted himself with eternity, and the utmost extent of the universe? For what is there in human knowledge, or the short span of this life, that can appear great to a wise man? whose mind is always so upon its guard, that nothing can befall him unforeseen, nothing unexpected, nothing new. Such a one takes so exact a survey on all sides of him, that he always knows how to dispose of himself, without anxiety, or any care about this world, and entertains every accident that befalls him with a becoming calmness. Whoever conducts himself in this manner, will be void of grief, and every other perturbation: and a mind free from these renders men completely happy: whereas a mind disordered and drawn off from right and unerring reason, loses at once, not only its resolution, but its health. Therefore the thoughts and declarations of the Peripatetics are soft and effeminate, for they say that the mind must necessarily be agitated, but confine it within a certain degree. And do you set bounds to vice? What! is not every disobedience to reason a vice? doth not reason sufficiently declare, that there is no real good which you should too ardently desire, or the possession of which should transport you; or any evil that should dispirit you, or that the suspicion of it should distract you? and that all these things assume too melancholy, or too cheerful an appearance through our own error? But if fools find this error lessened by time, so that, though the cause remains the same, they are not in the same manner, after some time, as they were at first affected; a wise man ought not to be influenced at all by it. But what are those degrees we are to limit it by? Let us fix these degrees in grief, a subject much canvassed. Fannius writes that P. Rutilius took it much to heart, that his brother was refused the consulate: but he seems to have been too much affected by it; for it was the occasion of his death: he ought therefore to have borne it with more moderation. But let us suppose, that whilst he bore this with moderation, the death of his children had intervened; here would have started a fresh grief, which, admitting it to be moderate in itself, yet still it would be a great addition to the other. Now to these let us add some acute pains of body, the loss of his fortunes, blindness, banishment; supposing then each misfortune to occasion an additional grief, the whole would be insupportable.

XVIII. The man who attempts to set bounds to vice, acts like one who should throw himself headlong from Leucate, persuaded he could stop himself whenever he pleased. Now, as that is impossible, so a perturbed and disordered mind cannot refrain itself, and stop where it pleases. Certainly whatever is bad in its increase, is bad in its birth: now grief, and all other perturbations, are doubtless baneful in their progress, and have therefore no small share of infection at the beginning; for they go on of themselves when once they depart from reason, for every weakness is self-indulgent, and indiscreetly launches out, and doth not know where to stop. Wherefore the difference is small betwixt approving of moderate perturbations of mind, and moderate injustice, moderate cowardice, moderate intemperance. For whoever prescribes bounds to vice, admits of a part of it, which, as it is odious of itself, becomes the more so as it stands on slippery ground, and being once set forward, slides headlong, and cannot by any means be stopped.

XIX. But what if the Peripatetics, whilst we say that these perturbations should be extirpated, not only say they are natural, but that they were given by nature to a good purpose. They usually talk in this manner. In the first place, they say much in praise of anger; they call it the whetstone of courage, and they say that angry men exert themselves most against an enemy or bad citizen: that those reasons are of little weight which depend on reflection; such as, it is a just war, it becomes us to fight for our laws, our liberties, our country; they will allow no force in these, unless our courage is warmed by anger. Nor do they confine their argument to warriors: but their opinion is, that no one can issue any rigid commands without some mixture of anger. In short, they have no notion, even of an orator either accusing or defending, without being spurred on by anger. And though it should not be real, they think his words and gesture must carry the appearance of it, that the action of the orator may excite this passion in his hearer. And they deny that any man was ever seen, who doth not know what it is to be angry: and they name what we call lenity, by the bad appellation of indolence: nor do they commend only this lust, (for anger is, as I defined it above, the lust of revenge,) but they maintain that kind of lust or desire to be given us by nature for very good purposes: that no one can execute any thing well but what he is in earnest about. Themistocles used to walk in the public places in the night, because he could not sleep: and when asked the reason, his answer was, that Miltiades' trophies kept him awake. Who has not heard how Demosthenes used to watch? who said it gave him pain, if any mechanic was up in a morning at his work before him. Lastly, that some of the greatest philosophers had never made that progress in their studies, but from an ardent desire. We are informed that Pythagoras, Democritus, and Plato visited the remotest parts of the world; they thought that they ought to go wherever any thing was to be learned. Now it is not conceivable that these things could be effected but by the greatest ardour of mind.

XX. They say that even grief, which we describe as a monstrous fierce beast, and to be avoided as such, was appointed by nature, not without some good purpose: that men should lament when they had committed a fault, well knowing they had exposed themselves to correction, rebuke, and ignominy. For they think those who can bear ignominy and infamy without pain, are at liberty to commit what crimes they please: for with them, reproach is a stronger check than conscience. From whence we have that in Afranius, borrowed from common life; for when the abandoned son saith, Wretched that I am! the severe father replies,

Let him but grieve, no matter what the cause.

And they say the other diseases of the mind have their use; pity incites us to the assistance of others, and to alleviate the calamities of men, who undeservedly fall into them: that even envy and defamation are not without their use; as when you see one attain what you cannot, or observe another on a footing with yourself: that, should you take away fear, you would supplant all diligence in life; which those use most who are afraid of the laws and the magistrates, who dread poverty, ignominy, death, and pain. But when they argue thus, they allow of their being retrenched, though they deny that they either can, or should be plucked up by the roots: so that their opinion is, that mediocrity is best in every thing. When they reason in this manner, what think you? do they say something or nothing? *A.* To me they say something; I wait therefore to hear what you will say to them.

XXI. *M.* Perhaps I may find something: but this first; do you take notice with what modesty the Academics behave themselves? for they speak plainly to the purpose. The Peripatetics are answered by the Stoics; they have my leave to fight it out; who think myself no otherwise concerned than to inquire after probabilities. The business is, then, if we can meet with any thing in this question that touches on the probable, beyond which human nature cannot proceed. The definition of a perturbation, as Zeno, I think, has rightly determined it, is thus: That a perturbation is a commotion of the mind against nature, in opposition to right reason; or shorter thus, that a perturbation is a more vehement appetite; that is called more vehement which is at a greater distance from the constant course of nature. What can I say to these definitions? the most part of them we have from those who dispute with sagacity and acuteness: some indeed, such as the "ardours of the mind," and "the whetstones of virtue," savour of the pomp of rhetoricians. As to the question, if a brave man can maintain his courage without becoming angry; it may be questioned with regard to the gladiators: though we observe much resolution even in them; they meet, converse, they agree about terms, so that they seem rather placid than angry. But let us admit some Placideianus of that trade, to be in such a mind, as Lucilius relates of him:

> If for his blood you thirst, the task be mine;
> His laurels at my feet he shall resign;
> Not but I know, before I reach his heart,
> First on myself a wound he will impart.
> I hate the man; enrag'd I fight, and straight
> In action we had been, but that I wait
> Till each his sword had fitted to his hand,
> My rage I scarce can keep within command.

XXII. But we see Ajax in Homer advancing to meet Hector in battle cheerfully, without any of this boisterous wrath, who had no sooner taken up his arms, but the first step he made inspired his associates with joy, his enemies with fear: that even Hector, as he is represented by Homer, trembling, condemned himself for having challenged him to fight. Yet these conversed together, calmly and quietly, before they engaged; nor did they shew any anger, or outrageous behaviour during the combat. Nor do I imagine that Torquatus, the first who obtained this surname, was in a rage, when he plundered the Gaul of his collar: or that Marcellus's courage at Clastidium was owing to his anger. I could almost swear, that Africanus, whom we are better acquainted with, from the freshness of his memory, was no ways inflamed by anger, when he covered Alienus Pelignus with his shield, and drove his sword into the enemy's breast. There may be some doubt of L. Brutus, if, through infinite hatred of the tyrant, he might not attack Aruns with more rashness, for I observed they mutually killed each other in close fight. Why then do you call in the assistance of anger? would courage, should it not begin to madden, lose its energy? What? do you imagine Hercules, whom the very courage, which you would have to be anger, preferred to heaven, was angry when he engaged the Erymanthian boar, or the Nemean lion? or was Theseus in a passion when he seized on the horns of the Marathonian bull? Take care how you make courage to depend in the least on rage; when anger is altogether irrational, and that is not courage which is void of reason.

XXIII. We ought to hold all things here in contempt; death is to be looked on with indifference; pains and labours as tolerable. When these are established on judgment and conviction, then will that stout and firm courage take place; unless you attribute to anger whatever is done with vehemence, alacrity, and spirit. To me indeed that very Scipio who was chief-priest, that favourer of the saying of the Stoics, "that no private man could be a wise man," doth not seem to be angry with Tiberius Gracchus, even when he left the consul in a languishing condition, and, though a private man himself, commanded, with the authority of a consul, that all who meant well to the republic should follow him. I do not know whether I have done any thing in the republic that has the appearance of courage; but if I have, I certainly did not do it in wrath. Doth any thing come nearer madness than anger? which Ennius has well defined, the beginning of madness. The changing colour, the alteration of our voice, the look of our eyes, our manner of fetching our breath, the little command we have over our words and actions, how little do they partake of a sound mind! What can make a worse appearance than Homer's Achilles, or Agamemnon, during the quarrel? And as to Ajax, anger drove him into downright madness, and was the occasion of his death. Courage therefore doth not want the patronage of anger; it is sufficiently provided, armed, and prepared of itself. We may as well say that drunkenness, or madness, is of service to courage, because those who are mad or drunk do a great many things often with more vehemence. Ajax was always brave, but most so when in a passion:

> The greatest feat that Ajax e'er achiev'd
> Was when his single arm the Greeks relieved.
> Quitting the field; urg'd on by rising rage,
> Forc'd the declining troops again t' engage.

XXIV. Shall we say then that madness has its use? Examine the definitions of courage: you will find it doth not require the assistance of passion. Courage is, then, an affection of the mind, that bears all things with subjection to the chief law; or a firm maintenance of judgment in supporting or repelling every thing that has a formidable appearance, or knowing what is formidable or otherwise, and by maintaining invariably such a sense of them, as to bear them, or despise them; or, in fewer words, according to Chrysippus: (for the above definition are Sphærus's, one of the first ability in defining, as the Stoics think: but they are all pretty much alike, they give us only common notions, some one way, and some another.) But what is Chrysippus's definition? Fortitude, saith he, is the knowledge of all things that are bearable: or an affection of the mind, which bears and supports every thing in obedience to the chief law of reason, without fear. Now, though we should take the same liberty with these, as Carneades used to do, I fear they will be the only philosophers: for which of these definitions doth not explain that obscure and intricate notion of courage which every man conceives within himself? which being thus explained, what can a warrior, a commander, or an orator, want more? and no one can think but that they will behave themselves courageously without anger. What? do not even the Stoics, who maintain that all fools are mad, make the same inferences? for take away perturbations, especially a hastiness of temper, and they will appear to talk very absurdly. But what they assert is thus: they say that all fools are mad, as all dunghills stink; not that they always do so, but stir them, and you will perceive it. Thus a hot man is not always in a passion; but provoke him, and you will see him run mad. Now, that very anger, which is of such service in war, what is its use at home with his wife, children, and family? Is there, then, any thing that a perturbed mind can do better than that which is calm and steady? or can any one be angry without a perturbation of mind? Our people then were in the right, who, as all vices depend on our morals, and nothing is worse than a testy disposition, called angry men alone morose.

XXV. Anger is in no wise becoming in an orator; it is not amiss to affect it. Do you imagine I am angry when I plead with unusual vehemence and sharpness? What? when I write out my speeches after all is over and past? Or do you think Æsopus was ever angry when he acted, or Accius was so when he wrote? They act indeed very well, but the orator better than the player, provided he be really an orator: but then they carry it on without passion, and with a composed mind. But what wantonness is it to commend lust? You produce Themistocles and Demosthenes: to these you add Pythagoras, Democritus, and Plato. What, do you call studies lust? Now should these studies be of the most excellent turn, as those were which you mentioned, they ought however to be composed and tranquil: and what kind of philosophers are they who commend grief, than which nothing is more detestable? Afranius has said much to their purpose,

Let him but grieve, no matter what the cause.

But he spoke this of a debauched and dissolute youth: but we are inquiring after a constant and wise man. We may even allow a centurion, or standard-bearer, to be angry, or any others, whom, not to explain the mysteries of the rhetoricians, I shall not mention here, for to touch the passions, where reason cannot be come at, may have its use; but my inquiry, as I often aver, is of a wise man.

XXVI. But even envy, detraction, pity, have their use. Why should you pity rather than assist, if it is in your power? Is it because you cannot be liberal without pity? We should not take cares on ourselves upon another's account; but ease others of their grief if we can. But that detraction, or that vicious emulation, which resembles a rivalship, of what use is it? Now envy implies being uneasy at another's good, and that because he enjoys it. How can it be right, that you should voluntarily grieve, rather than take the trouble of acquiring what you want to have; for it is madness in the highest degree, to desire to be the only one that has it. But who can with correctness speak in praise of a mediocrity of evils? Can any one in whom there is lust or desire, be otherwise than libidinous or desirous? or not be angry, where any vexation is, not to be vexed? or where fear is, not to be fearful? Do we look then on the libidinous, the angry, the anxious, and the timid man, as persons of wisdom? of whose excellence I could speak very largely and copiously, but wish to be as short as possible. Thus, that wisdom is an acquaintance with all divine and human affairs, or a knowledge of the cause of every thing. Hence it is, that it imitates what is divine, and holds all human concerns as inferior to virtue. Did you then say, that it was your opinion that such a man was as naturally liable to perturbation as the sea is exposed to winds? What is there that can discompose such gravity and constancy? Any thing sudden or unforeseen? How can any thing of this kind befall one, to whom nothing is sudden that can happen to man? Now, as to their saying that redundancies should be pared off, and only what is natural remain; what, I pray you, can be natural, which may be too exuberant? All these proceed from the roots of errors, which must be entirely plucked up and destroyed, not pared and lopt off.

XXVII. But as I suspect that your inquiry is more with regard to yourself than the wise man, for you allow him to be free from all perturbations, and would willingly yourself be so too; let us see what remedies may be applied by philosophy to the diseases of the mind. There is certainly some remedy; nor has nature been so unkind to the human race, as to have discovered so many salutary things for the body, and none for the mind. She has even been kinder to the mind than the body; inasmuch as you must seek abroad for the assistance the body requires; the mind has all within itself. But by how much more excellent and divine the mind is, it requires the more diligence; which, when it is well applied, it discovers what is best; when neglected, is involved in many errors. I shall apply then all my discourse to you; for though you appear to inquire about the wise man, your inquiry may possibly be about yourself. Various, then, are the cures of those perturbations which I have expounded; for every disorder is not to be appeased the same way;—one medicine must be applied to one who mourns, another to the pitiful, another to the person who envies; for there is this difference to be maintained in all the four perturbations: we are to consider, whether the cure is to be applied, as to a perturbation in general, that is, a contempt of reason, or vehement appetite; or whether it would be better directed to particular perturbations, as to fear, lust, and the rest: whether that is not to be much affected by that which occasioned the grief, or whether every kind of grief is not to be entirely set aside. As, should any one grieve that he is poor, the question is, would you maintain poverty to be no evil, or would you contend that a man ought not to grieve at any thing? Certainly this is best; for should you not convince him with regard to poverty, you must allow him to grieve: but if you remove grief by particular arguments, such as I used yesterday, the evil of poverty is in some manner removed.

XXVIII. But any perturbation of the mind of this sort may be, as it were, wiped away by this method of appeasing the mind: by shewing that there is no good in what gave rise to joy and lust, nor any evil in what occasioned fear or grief. But certainly the most effectual cure is, by shewing that all perturbations are of themselves vicious, and have nothing natural or necessary in them. As we see grief itself is easily softened, when we charge those who grieve with weakness, and an effeminate mind: or when we commend the gravity and constancy of those who bear calmly whatever befalls them here, which indeed is generally the case with those who look on these as real evils, but yet think they should be borne with resignation. One imagines pleasure to be a good, another money; and yet the one may be called off from intemperance, the other from covetousness. The other method and address, which, at the same time that it removes the false opinion, withdraws the disorder, has more subtilty in it: but it seldom succeeds, and is not applicable to vulgar minds, for there are some diseases which that medicine can by no means remove. For should any one be uneasy that he is without virtue, without courage, void of duty, or honesty; his anxiety proceeds from a real evil, and yet we must apply another method of cure to him; and such a one as all the philosophers, however they may differ about other things, agree in. For they must necessarily consent to this, that commotions of the mind in opposition to right reason are vicious: that, even admitting those things not to be evils, which occasion fear or grief; nor those good which provoke desire or joy, yet that very commotion itself is vicious; for we mean by the expressions magnanimous and brave, one who is resolute, sedate, grave, and superior to every thing in this life: but one who either grieves, fears, covets, or is transported with passion, cannot come under that denomination; for these things are consistent only with those who look on the things of this world as an overmatch for their minds.

XXIX. Wherefore, as I before said, the philosophers have all one method of cure; that nothing is to be said to that, whatever it is, that disturbs the mind, but concerning the perturbation itself. Thus, first, with regard to desire; when the business is only to remove that, the inquiry is not to be, whether that be good or evil, which provokes lust; but lust itself is to be removed: so that, whether honesty be the chief good, or pleasure, or whether it consists in both these together, or in the other three kinds of goods, yet, should there be in any one too vehement an appetite of even virtue itself, the whole discourse should be directed to the deterring him from that vehemence. But human nature, when placed in a conspicuous view, gives us every argument for appeasing the mind; and to make this the more distinct, the law and conditions of life should be explained in our discourse. Therefore it was not without reason, that Socrates is reported, when Euripides acquainted him with his play, called Orestes, to have begged that the three first verses might be repeated:

> What tragic story men can mournful tell,
> Whate'er from fate or from the gods befell,
> That human nature can support . . . . .

But in order to persuade those to whom any misfortune has happened, that they can and ought to bear it, it is very useful to set before them others who have borne the like. Indeed the method of appeasing grief was explained in my dispute of yesterday, and in my book of Consolation, which I wrote in the midst of my own grief, for I was not the wise man: and applied this, notwithstanding Chrysippus's advice to the contrary, who is against applying a medicine to the fresh swellings of the mind: but I did it, and committed a violence on nature, that the greatness of my grief might give way to the greatness of the medicine.

XXX. But fear borders upon grief, of which I have

already said enough: but I must say a little more on that. Now, as grief proceeds from what is present, so fear from future evil: so that some have said that fear is a certain part of grief: others have called fear the harbinger of trouble; which, as it were, introduces the ensuing evil. Now the reasons that make what is present tolerable, make what is to come of little weight: for with regard to both, we should take care to do nothing low or grovelling, soft or effeminate, mean or abject. But notwithstanding we should speak of the inconstancy, imbecility, and levity of fear itself, yet it is of greater service to despise those very things we are afraid of. So that it fell out very well, whether it was by accident or design, that I disputed the first and second day on death and pain; two things that are the most dreaded: now, if what I then said was approved of, we are in a great degree freed from fear. And thus far on the opinion of evils.

XXXI. Proceed we now to goods, i. e. joy and desire. To me, indeed, one thing alone seems to take in the cause of all that relates to the perturbations of the mind; that all perturbations are in our own power; that they are taken up upon opinion; and are voluntary. This error then must be discharged; this opinion removed: and, as with regard to imagined evils, we are to make them more tolerable, so with respect to goods, we are to lessen the violent effects of those things which are called great and joyous. But one thing is to be observed, that equally relates both to good and evil: that should it be difficult to persuade any one, that none of those things which disturb the mind are to be looked on as good or evil, yet a different cure is to be applied to different motions; and the malevolent person is to be corrected by one way of reasoning, the lover by another, the anxious man by another, and the fearful by another: and it were easy for any one who pursues the best approved method of reasoning, with regard to good and evil, to maintain that no fool can be affected with joy, as he never can have any thing good. But, at present, my discourse proceeds upon the common received notions. Let, then, honours, riches, pleasures, and the rest, be the very good things they are imagined; yet a too elevated and exulting joy on the possessing them is unbecoming; for, though it were allowable to laugh, a loud laugh would be indecent. Thus a mind enlarged by joy, is as blameable as a contraction of it in grief: and longing is of equal levity with the joy of possessing; and as those who are too dejected are said to be effeminate, so they who are too elate with joy, are properly called volatile: and as envy partakes of grief, so to be pleased with another's misfortune, or joy; and both these are usually corrected, by shewing the wildness and insensibility of them. And as it becomes a man to be cautious, but it is unbecoming to be fearful; so to be pleased is proper, but to be joyful improper. I have, that I might be the better understood, distinguished pleasure from joy. I have already said above, that a contraction of the mind can never be right, but an elation may: for the joy of Hector in Nævius is one thing,

'Tis joy indeed to hear my praises sung
By you, who are the theme of honour's tongue;

but that of the character in Trabea another, " The kind procuress, allured by my money, will observe my nod, will watch my desires, and study my will. If I but move the door with my little finger, instantly it flies open; and if Chrysis should unexpectedly discover me, she will run with joy to meet me, and throw herself into my arms." Now he will tell you how excellent he thinks this:

Not even fortune herself is so fortunate.

XXXII. Any one who attends the least to it will be convinced how unbecoming this joy is. And as they are very shameful, who are immoderately delighted with the enjoyment of venereal pleasures; so are they very scandalous, who lust vehemently after them. And all that which is commonly called love (and believe me I can find out no other name to call it by) is of such levity, that nothing, I think, is to be compared to it; of which Cæcilius:

> I hold the man of every sense bereav'd,
> Who grants not love to be of gods the chief;
> Whose mighty power whate'er is good effects,
> Who gives to each his beauty and defects:
> Hence health and sickness; wit and folly hence,
> The God that love and hatred doth dispense!

An excellent corrector of life this same poetry! which thinks that love, the promoter of debauchery and vanity, should have a place in the council of the gods. I am speaking of comedy: which could not subsist at all, but on our approving of these debaucheries. But what said that chief of the Argonauts in tragedy?

> My life I owe to honour less than love.

What then? this love of Medea, what a train of miseries did it occasion! and yet the same woman has the assurance to say to her father, in another poet, that she had a husband

> Dearer by love than ever fathers were.

XXXIII. But let us allow the poets to trifle: in whose fables we see Jupiter himself engaged in these debaucheries: apply we then to the masters of virtue, the philosophers who deny love to be any thing carnal; and in this they differ from Epicurus, who, I think, is not much mistaken. For what is that love of friendship? How comes it, that no one is in love with a deformed young man, or a handsome old one? I am of opinion, that this love of men had its rise from the gymnastics of the Greeks, where these kinds of loves are free and allowed of: therefore Ennius spoke well;

The censure of this crime to those is due,
Who naked bodies first expos'd to view.

Now supposing them chaste, which I think is hardly possible; they are uneasy and distressed, and the more so, as they contain and refrain themselves. But to pass over the love of women, where nature has allowed more liberty; who can misunderstand the poets in their rape of Ganymede, or not apprehend what Laius saith, and what he would be at, in Euripides? Lastly, what the principal poets and the most learned have published of themselves in their poems and songs? What doth Alcus, who was distinguished in his own republic for his bravery, write on the love of young men? and all Anacreon's poetry is on love. But Ibycus of Rhegium appears, from his writings, to have had this love stronger on him than all the rest.

XXXIV. Now we see that the loves of these were libidinous. There have arisen some amongst us philosophers (and Plato is at the head of them, whom Dicæarchus blames not without reason) who have countenanced love. The Stoics in truth say, not only that their wise man may be a lover, but they also define love itself to be an endeavour of making friendship from the appearance of beauty. Now, provided there is any one in the nature of things, without desire, without care, without a sigh; such a one may be a lover: for he is free from all lust: but I have nothing to say to him, as lust is my subject. But should there be any love, as there certainly is, which is but little short, if at all, of madness, such as his in the Leucadia,

> Should there be any god whose care I am;

it is incumbent on all the gods to see that he enjoys his amorous pleasure.

> Wretch that I am!

Nothing truer, and he saith very well.

> What, are you sane, lamenting at this rate?

He seems even to his friends to be out of his senses: then how tragical he becomes!

> Thy aid, divine Apollo, I implore,
> And thine, dread ruler of the wat'ry store!
> Oh! all ye winds, assist me!

He thinks the whole world should be overturned to help his love: he excludes Venus alone as unkind to him. "Thy aid, O Venus, why should I invoke?" He thinks Venus too much employed in her own lust, to have regard to any thing else, as if he himself had not said, and committed these shameful things from lust.

XXXV. Now the cure for one affected in this manner, is to shew, how light, how contemptible, how very trifling he is in what he desires; how he may turn his affections to another object, or accomplish his desires by some other means, or that he may entirely disregard it; sometimes he is to be led away to things of another kind, to study, business, or other different engagements and concerns: very often the cure is effected by change of place, as sick people, that have not recovered their strength. Some think an old love may be driven out by a new one, as one nail drives out another: but he should be principally advised, what madness love is: for of all the perturbations of the mind, nothing is more vehement; though, without charging it with rapes, debaucheries, adultery, or even incest, the baseness of any of these being very blameable; yet, I say, not to mention these, the very perturbation of the mind in love, is base of itself; for, to pass over all its mad tricks, those very things which are looked on as indifferent, what weakness do they argue? "Affronts, jealousies, jars, parleys, wars, then peace again. Now, for you to ask advice to love by, is all one as if you should ask advice to run mad by." Now is not this inconstancy and mutability of mind enough to deter one by its own deformity? We are to demonstrate, as was said of every perturbation, that it consists entirely in opinion and judgment, and is owing to ourselves. For if love were natural, all would be in love, and always so, and love the same object; nor would one be deterred by shame, another by reflection, another by satiety.

XXXVI. Anger, too, when it disturbs the mind any time, leaves no room to doubt its being madness: by the instigation of which, we see such contention as this between brothers:

> Where was there ever impudence like thine?
> Who on thy malice ever could refine?

You know what follows: for abuses are thrown out by these brothers, with great bitterness, in every other verse; so that you may easily know them for the sons of Atreus, of that Atreus who invented a new punishment for his brother:

> I, who his cruel heart to gall am bent,
> Some new, unheard-of torment must invent.

Now what were these inventions? Hear Thyestes:

> My impious brother fain would have me eat
> My children, and thus serves them up for meat.

To what length now will not anger go? even as far as madness. Therefore we say properly enough, that angry men have given up their power, that is, they are out of the power of advice, reason, and understanding: for these ought to have power over the whole mind. Now you should put those out of the way, whom they endeavour to attack, till they have recollected themselves; but what doth recollection here imply, but getting together the dispersed parts of their mind? or they are to be begged and entreated, if they have the means of revenge, to defer it to another opportunity, till their anger cools. But the expression of cooling implies, certainly, that there was a heat raised there in opposition to reason: from whence that saying of Archytas is commended; who being somewhat provoked at his steward, "How would I have treated you," saith he, "if I had not been in a passion?"

XXXVII. Where then are they who say that anger has its use? Can madness be of any use? But still it is natural. Can any thing be natural that is against reason? or how is it, if anger is natural, that one is more inclined to anger than another? or how is it, that the lust of revenge should cease before it has revenged itself? or that any one should repent of what he had done in a passion? as we see Alexander could scarce keep his hands from himself, when he had killed his favourite Clytus: so great was his compunction! Now who, that is acquainted with these, can doubt but that this motion of the mind is altogether in opinion and voluntary? for who can doubt but that disorders of the mind, such as covetousness, a desire of glory, arise from a great estimation of those things by which the mind is disordered? from whence we may understand, that every perturbation is founded in opinion. And if boldness, i. e. a firm assurance of mind, is a kind of knowledge and serious opinion, not hastily taken up: then diffidence is a fear of an expected and impending evil: and if hope is an expectation of good, fear must of course be an expectation of evil. Thus fear and other perturbations are evils. Therefore as constancy proceeds from knowledge, so perturbation from error. Now they who are said to be naturally inclined to anger, or pitiful, or envious, or any thing of this kind; their minds are constitutionally, as it were, in bad health, yet they are curable, as is said of Socrates, when Zopyrus, who professed knowing the nature of every one from his person, had heaped a great many vices on him in a public assembly, he was laughed at by others, who could perceive no such vices in Socrates: but Socrates kept him in countenance, by declaring that such vices were natural to him, but he had got the better of them by his reason. Therefore, as any one who has the appearance of the best constitution, may yet be more inclined to some particular disorder, so different minds may be differently inclined to different diseases. But those who are said to be vicious, not by nature, but their own fault; their vices proceed from wrong opinions of good and bad things, so that one is more prone than another to different motions and perturbations. And so in the body, an inveterate disorder is harder to be got rid of than a perturbation; and a fresh tumour in the eyes is sooner cured than a defluxion of any continuance is removed.

XXXVIII. But as the cause of perturbations is discovered, all which arise from the judgment or opinion, and volitions, I shall put an end to this discourse. But we ought to be assured, the ends of good and evil being discovered, as far as they are discoverable by man, that nothing can be desired of philosophy greater, or more useful, than what I have disputed of these four days. For to a contempt of death, and the few enabled to bear pain, I have added the appeasing of grief, than which there is no greater evil to man. Though every perturbation of mind is grievous, and differs but little from madness; yet we are used to say of others, when they are under any perturbation, as of fear, joy, or desire, that they are moved and disturbed; but of those who give themselves up to grief, that they are miserable, afflicted, wretched, unhappy. So that it doth not seem to be by accident, but with reason proposed by you, that I should dispute separately of grief, and of the other perturbations; for there lies the spring and head of all our miseries: but the cure of grief, and of other disorders, is one and the same, in that they are all voluntary, and founded on opinion; we take them on ourselves because it seems right so to do. Philosophy promises to pluck up this error, as the root of all our evils: let us surrender ourselves to be instructed by it, and suffer ourselves to be cured; for whilst these evils have possession of us, we not only cannot be happy, but cannot be right in our minds. We must either deny that reason can effect any thing, while, on the other hand, nothing can be done right without reason; or, since philosophy depends on the deductions of reason, we must seek from her, if we would be good or happy, every help and assistance for living well and happily.

BOOK V.

WHETHER VIRTUE ALONE BE SUFFICIENT FOR A HAPPY LIFE.

This fifth day, Brutus, shall put an end to our Tusculan Disputations: on which day I disputed on your favourite subject. For I perceived from that accurate book you wrote me, as well as from your frequent conversation, that you are clearly of this opinion, that virtue is of itself sufficient for a happy life: and though it may be difficult to prove this, on account of the many various strokes of fortune, yet it is a truth of such a nature, that we should endeavour to facilitate the proof of it. For among all the topics of philosophy, there is none of more dignity or importance. As the first philosophers must have had some inducement, to neglect every thing for the search of the best state of life; surely it was with the hopes of living happily, that they laid out so much care and pains on that study. Now, if virtue was discovered and carried to perfection by them; and if virtue is a sufficient security for a happy life; who but must think the work of philosophising excellently established by them, and undertaken by me? But if virtue, as subject to such various and uncertain accidents, is but the slave of fortune, and not of sufficient ability to support herself; I am afraid we should seem rather to offer up our petitions to her, than endeavour to place our confidence in virtue for a happy life. Indeed, when I reflect on those troubles with which I have been severely exercised by fortune, I begin to suspect this opinion, and sometimes even to dread the weakness and frailty of human nature; for I am afraid, lest as nature has given us infirm bodies, and has joined to these incurable diseases and intolerable pains, she might also have given us minds participating of these bodily pains, and harassed with troubles and uneasinesses peculiarly her own. But here I correct myself, for forming my judgment of the force of virtue, more from the weakness of others, or mine own perhaps, than from virtue itself: for that (provided there is such a thing as virtue, and your uncle Brutus has removed all doubt of it) has every thing that can befall man in subjection to her; and by disregarding them, is not at all concerned at human accidents: and being free from every imperfection, thinks nothing beyond herself can relate to her. But we, who increase every approaching evil by our fear, and every present one by our grief, choose rather to condemn the nature of things, than our own errors.

II. But the amendment of this fault, and of all our other vices and offences, is to be sought for in philosophy: to whose protection as my own inclination and desire led me, from my earliest days, so, under my present misfortunes, I have recourse to the same port, from whence I set out, after having been tossed by a violent tempest. O Philosophy, thou conductor of life! thou discoverer of virtue, and expeller of vices! what had not only I myself been, but the whole life of man, without you? To you we owe the origin of cities; you called together the dispersed race of men into social life; you united them together, first, by placing them near one another, then by marriages, and lastly by the communication of speech and languages. To you we owe the invention of laws; you instructed us in morals and discipline. To you I fly for assistance; and as I formerly submitted to you in a great degree, so now I surrender up myself entirely to you. For one day well spent, and agreeably to your precepts, is preferable to an eternity of sin. Whose assistance then can be of more service to me than yours, which has bestowed on us tranquillity of life, and removed the fear of death? But philosophy is so far from being praised, as she hath deserved of man, that she is wholly neglected by most, and ill spoken of by many. Can any speak ill of the parent of life, and dare to pollute himself thus with parricide! and be so impiously ungrateful as to accuse her, whom he ought to reverence, had he been less acquainted with her? But this error, I imagine, and this darkness, has spread itself over the minds of ignorant men, from their not being able to look so far back, and from their not imagining that those by whom human life was first improved, were philosophers: for though we see philosophy to have been of long standing, yet the name must be acknowledged to be but modern.

III. But, indeed, who can dispute the antiquity of philosophy, either in fact or name? which acquired this excellent name from the ancients, by the knowledge of the origin and causes of every thing, both divine and human. Thus those seven Σοφοι, as they were held and called by the Greeks, and wise men by us: and thus Lycurgus many ages before, in whose time, before the building of this city, Homer is said to have been, as well as Ulysses and Nestor in the heroic ages were all reported really to have been, as they were called, wise men; nor would it have been said, that Atlas supported the heavens, or that Prometheus was bound to Caucasus, nor would Cepheus, with his wife, his son-in-law, and his daughter, have been enrolled among the constellations, but that their more than human knowledge of the heavenly bodies had transferred their names into an erroneous fable. From whence, all who were exercised in the contemplation of nature were held to be, as well as called, wise men: and that name of theirs continued to the age of Pythagoras, who is reported to have gone to Phlius, as we find it in Ponticus Heraclides, a very learned man, and a hearer of Plato's, and to have discoursed very learnedly and copiously on certain subjects with Leon, prince of the Phliasii. Leon, admiring his ingenuity and eloquence, asked him what art he particularly professed? his answer was, that he was acquainted with no art, but that he was a philosopher. Leon, surprised at the novelty of the name, inquired what he meant by the name of philosopher, and in what they differed from other men? on which Pythagoras replied, "That the life of man seemed to him to resemble those games which were kept with the greatest entertainment of sports, and the general concourse of all Greece. For as there were some, whose pursuit was glory, and the honour of a crown, for the performance of bodily exercises; so others were induced by the gain of buying and selling, and mere lucrative motives: but there was likewise one sort of them, and they by far the best, whose aim was neither applause, nor profit, but who came merely as spectators through curiosity, to remark what was done, and to see in what manner things were carried on there. Thus we come from another life and nature unto this, as it were out of another city, to some much frequented mart; some slaves to glory, others to money: that there are some few, who, taking no account of any thing else, earnestly look into the nature of things: that these call themselves studious of wisdom, that is, philosophers; and as there it is more reputable to be a looker on, without making any acquisition, so in life, the contemplating on things, and acquainting yourself with them, greatly exceeds every other pursuit of life."

IV. Nor was Pythagoras the inventor only of the name, but he enlarged also the thing itself, and, when he came into Italy after this conversation at Phlius, adorned that Greece, which is called Great Greece, both privately and publicly, with the most excellent institutes and arts; of whose discipline, perhaps, I shall find another opportunity to speak. But numbers and motions, the beginning and end of things, were the subjects of the ancient philosophy down to Socrates, who was a hearer of Archelaus, the disciple of Anaxagoras. These made diligent inquiry into the magnitude of the stars, their distances, courses, and all that relates to the heavens. But Socrates was the first who brought down philosophy from the heavens, placed it in cities, introduced it into families, and obliged it to examine into life and morals, good and evil. Whose several methods of disputing, together with the variety of his topics, and the greatness of his abilities, being immortalized by the memory and writings of Plato, gave rise to many sects of philosophers of different sentiments: of all which I have principally adhered to that, which, in my opinion, Socrates himself followed; to conceal my own opinion, clear others from their errors, and to discover what has the most probability in every question. A custom Carneades maintained with great copiousness and acuteness, and which I myself have often used on many occasions elsewhere; agreeable to which manner I disputed too in my Tusculum, and indeed I have sent you a book of the four former days' disputations; but the fifth day, when we had seated ourselves as before, what we were to dispute on was proposed thus.

V. *A.* I do not think virtue can possibly be sufficient to a happy life. *M.* But my Brutus thinks so, whose judgment, with submission, I greatly prefer to yours. *A.* I make no doubt of it; but your regard for him is not the business now, but what I said was my opinion: I wish you to dispute on that. *M.* What! do you deny that virtue can possibly be sufficient for a happy life? *A.* It is what I entirely deny. *M.* What! is not virtue sufficient to enable us to live as we ought, honestly, commendably, or, in fine, to live well? *A.* Certainly sufficient. *M.* Can you then help calling any one miserable, who lives ill? or any one whom you allow to live well, will you deny to live happily? *A.* Why may

I not? for a man may be upright in his life, honest, praiseworthy, and therefore live well, even in the midst of torments, but a happy life doth not aspire after that. *M.* What then? is your happy life left on the outside of the prison, whilst constancy, gravity, wisdom, and the other virtues, are surrendered up to the executioner, and bear punishment and pain without reluctance? *A.* You must look out for something new, if you would do any good. These things have very little effect on me, not merely from their being common, but principally because, like certain light wines, that will not bear water, these arguments of the Stoics are pleasanter to taste than to swallow. As when the assemblage of virtue is committed to the rack, it raises so reverend a spectacle before our eyes, that happiness seems to hasten on, and not to suffer them to be deserted by her. But when you take your attention off from these fancies, to the truth and the reality, what remains without disguise is, whether any one can be happy in torment. Wherefore let us examine that, and not be under any apprehensions, lest the virtues should expostulate and complain, that they are forsaken by happiness. For if prudence is connected with every virtue, prudence itself discovers this, that all good men are not therefore happy; and she recollects many things of M. Attilius, Q. Cæpio, M. Aquilius: and prudence herself, if these representations are more agreeable to you than the things themselves, pulls back happiness, when it is endeavouring to throw itself into torments, and denies that it has any connection with pain and torture.

VI. *M.* I can easily bear with your behaving in this manner, though it is not fair in you to prescribe to me, how you would have me to dispute: but I ask you, if I effected any thing or nothing in the foregoing days?

A. Yes, something was done, some little matter indeed. *M.* But if that is the case, this question is routed, and almost put an end to. *A.* How so? *M.* Because turbulent motions and violent agitations of the mind, raised and elated by a rash impulse, getting the better of reason, leave no room for a happy life. For who that fears either pain or death, the one of which is always present, the other always impending, can be otherwise than miserable? Now supposing the same person, which is often the case, to be afraid of poverty, ignominy, infamy, weakness, or blindness; or, lastly, which doth not befall particular men, but often the most powerful nations, slavery; now can any one under the apprehensions of these be happy? What! if he not only dreads as future, but actually feels and bears them at present? Let us unite in the same person, banishment, mourning, the loss of children; whoever is in the midst of this affliction is worn with sickness; can he be otherwise than very miserable indeed? What reason can there be, why a man should not rightly enough be called miserable, that we see inflamed and raging with lust, coveting every thing with an insatiable desire, and the more pleasures he receives from any thing, still thirsting the more violently after them? And as to a man vainly elated, exulting with an empty joy, and boasting of himself without reason, is not he so much the more miserable, as he thinks himself the happier? Therefore, as these are miserable, so on the other hand they are happy, who are alarmed by no fears, wasted by no griefs, provoked by no lusts, melted by no languid pleasures that arise from vain and exulting joys. We look on the sea as calm when not the least breath of air disturbs its waves; so the placid and quiet state of the mind is discovered when unmoved by any perturbation. Now if there be any one who holds the power of fortune, and every thing human, every thing that can possibly befall any man, as tolerable, so as to be out of the reach of fear or anxiety; and should such a one covet nothing, and be lifted up by no vain joy of mind, what can prevent his being happy? and if these are the effects of virtue, why cannot virtue itself make men happy?

VII. *A.* One of these is undeniable, that they who are under no apprehensions, no ways uneasy, who covet nothing, are lifted up by no vain joy, are happy: therefore I grant you that; and the other I am not at liberty to dispute; for it was proved by your former disputations that a wise man was free from every perturbation of mind. *M.* Doubtless, then, the dispute is over. *A.* Almost, I think, indeed. *M.* But yet, that is more usual with the mathematicians than philosophers. For the geometricians, when they teach any thing, if what they had before taught relates to their present subject, they take that for granted, and already proved; and explain only what they had not written on before. The philosophers, whatever subject they have in hand, get every thing together that relates to it; notwithstanding they had disputed on it somewhere else. Were not that the case, why should the Stoics say so much on that question, whether virtue was abundantly sufficient to a happy life? when it would have been answer enough, that they had before taught, that nothing was good but what was honest: this being proved, the consequence would be, that virtue was sufficient to a happy life: and, as follows from the other, so if a happy life consists in virtue, nothing can be good but what is honest: but they do not act in this manner: for they have distinct books of honesty, and the chief good; for though it follows from the former, that virtue has power enough to make life happy, yet they treat the other distinctly; for every thing, especially of so great consequence, should be supported by arguments which belong to that alone. Have a care how you imagine philosophy to have uttered any thing more noble, or that she has promised any thing more fruitful or of greater consequence: for, good gods! doth she not engage, that she will so accomplish him who submits to her laws, as to be always armed against fortune, and to have every assurance within himself of living well and happily; that he shall, in one word, be for ever happy. But let us see what she will perform. In the meanwhile I look upon it as a great thing, that she has promised. For Xerxes, who was loaded with all the rewards and gifts of fortune, not satisfied with his armies of horse and foot, nor the multitude of his ships, nor his infinite treasure of gold, offered a reward to any one who could find out a new pleasure: which, when discovered, he was not satisfied with; nor can there ever be an end to lusts. I wish we could engage any one, by a reward, to produce something the better to establish us in this.

VIII. *A.* I wish so indeed: but I want a little information. For I allow, that in what you have stated, the one is the consequence of the other; that as, if what is honest be the only good, it must follow, that a happy life is the effect of virtue; so that if a happy life consists in virtue, nothing can be good but virtue. But your Brutus, on the authority of Aristo and Antiochus, doth not see this: for he thinks the case to be the same, even if there was any thing good besides virtue. *M.* What then? do you imagine I shall dispute against Brutus? *A.* You may do what you please: for it is not for me to prescribe what you shall do. *M.* How these things agree together shall be inquired somewhere else: for I frequently disputed that with Antiochus, and lately with

Aristo, when, as general, I lodged with him at Athens. For to me it seemed that no one could possibly be happy under any evil: but a wise man might be under evil, if there are any evils of body or fortune. These things were said, which Antiochus has inserted in his books in many places: that virtue itself was sufficient to make life happy, but not the happiest: and that many things are so called from the major part, though they do not include all, as strength, health, riches, honour, and glory: which are determined by their kind, not their number: thus a happy life is so called from its being in a great degree so, though it should fall short in some point. To clear this up, is not absolutely necessary at present, though it seems to be said without any great consistency: for I do not apprehend what is wanting to one that is happy, to make him happier; for if any thing be wanting, he cannot be so much as happy; and as to what they say, that every thing is called and looked upon from the greater part, may be admitted in some things. But when they allow three kinds of evils; when any one is oppressed with all the evils of two kinds, as with adverse fortune, and his body worn out and harassed with all sorts of pains, shall we say such a one is little short of a happy life, not to say, the happiest? This is what Theophrastus could not maintain: for when he had laid down, that stripes, torments, tortures, the ruin of one's country, banishment, the loss of children, had great influence as to living miserably and unhappily, he durst not use any high and lofty expressions, when he was so low and abject in his opinion.

IX. How right he was is not the question; he certainly was consistent. Therefore I am not for objecting to consequences where the premises are allowed of. But this most elegant and learned of all the philosophers is not taken to task when he asserts his three kinds of good; but he is attacked by all for that book which he wrote on a happy life, in which book he has many arguments, why one who is tortured and racked cannot be happy. For in that he is supposed to say, that such a one cannot reach a complete happy life. He nowhere indeed said so absolutely, but what he saith amounts to the same thing. Can I then find fault with him; to whom I allowed, that pains of body are evils, that the ruin of a man's fortunes is an evil, if he should say that every good man is not happy, when all those things which he reckons as evils may befall a good man? The same Theophrastus is found fault with by all the books and schools of the philosophers, for commending that sentence in his Callisthenes:

Fortune, not wisdom, rules the life of man.

They say, never did philosopher assert any thing so languid. They are right indeed in that: but I do not apprehend any thing could be more consistent: for if there are so many good things that depend on the body, so many foreign to it, that depend on chance and fortune, is it not consistent that fortune, who governs every thing, both what is foreign and what belongs to the body, has greater power than counsel? Or would we rather imitate Epicurus? who is often excellent in many things which he speaks, but quite indifferent how consistent, or to the purpose. He commends spare diet, and in that he speaks as a philosopher; but it is for Socrates or Antisthenes to say so, not one who confines all good to pleasure. He denies that any one can live pleasantly, unless he lives honestly, wisely, and justly. Nothing is more serious than this, nothing more becoming a philosopher, had he not applied this very thing, to live honestly, justly, and wisely, to pleasure. What better, than that fortune interferes but little with a wise man? But doth he talk thus, who had said that pain is the greatest evil, or the only evil, and who might be afflicted with the sharpest pains all over his body, even at the time he is vaunting himself the most against fortune? Which very thing, too, Metrodorus has said, but in better language: "I have prevented you, Fortune; I have caught you, and cut off every access, so that you cannot possibly reach me." This would be excellent in the mouth of Aristo the Chian, or Zeno the Stoic, who held nothing to be an evil but what was base; but for you, Metrodorus, to prevent the approaches of fortune, who confine all that is good to your bowels and marrow; you, who define the chief good by a firm habit of body, and a well assured hope of its continuance,—for you to cut off every access of fortune? Why, you may instantly be deprived of that good. Yet the simple are taken with these, and from such sentences great is the crowd of their followers.

X. But it is the duty of one who disputes accurately, to see not what is said, but what is said consistently. As in the opinion which is the subject of this disputation; I maintain that every good man is always happy; it is clear what I mean by good men: I call those both wise and good men, who are provided and adorned with every virtue. Let us see then who are to be called happy. I imagine, indeed, those, who are possessed of good without any allay of evil: nor is there any other notion connected with the word that expresses happiness, but an absolute enjoyment of good without any evil. Virtue cannot attain this, if there is any thing good besides itself: for a crowd of evils would present themselves, if we allow poverty, obscurity, humility, solitude, the loss of friends, acute pains of the body, the loss of health, weakness, blindness, the ruin of one's country, banishment, slavery, to be evils: for, to conclude, a wise man may be in all these and many others: for they are brought on by chance, which may attack a wise man; but if these are evils, who can maintain a wise man to be always happy, when all these may light on him at the same time? I therefore do not easily agree with my Brutus, nor our common masters, nor those ancient ones, Aristotle, Speusippus, Xenocrates, Polemon, who reckon all that I have mentioned above as evils, and yet they say that a wise man is always happy; who, if they are charmed with this beautiful and illustrious title, which would very well become Pythagoras, Socrates, and Plato, they should be persuaded, that strength, health, beauty, riches, honours, power, with the beauty of which they are ravished, are contemptible, and that all those things which are the opposites of these are not to be regarded. Then might they declare openly, with a loud voice, that neither the attacks of fortune, nor the opinion of the multitude, nor pain, nor poverty, occasion them any apprehensions; and that they have every thing within themselves, and that they hold nothing to be good but what is within their own power. Nor can I by any means allow the same person who falls into the vulgar opinion of good and evil, to make use of these expressions, which can only become a great and exalted man. Struck with which glory, up starts Epicurus, who, with submission to the gods, thinks a wise man always happy. He is much taken with the dignity of this opinion, but he never would have owned that, had he attended to himself: for what is there more inconsistent, than for one who could say that pain was the greatest or the only evil, to think that a wise man should say in the midst of his torture, How sweet is this! We are not therefore to form our judgment of philosophers from detached sentences, but from their consistency with themselves, and their common manner of talking.

XI. *A.* You engage me to be of your opinion; but have a care that you are not inconsistent yourself. *M.* By what means? *A.* Because I have lately read your fourth book on Good and Evil: in that you appeared to me, when disputing against Cato, to have endeavoured to shew, which with me is to prove, that Zeno and the Peripatetics differ only about some new words; which allowed, what reason can there be, if it follows from the arguments of Zeno, that virtue contains all that is necessary to a happy life, that the Peripatetics should not be at liberty to say the same? For, in my opinion, regard should be had to the thing, not to words. *M.* What? you would convict me from my own words, and bring against me what I had said or written elsewhere. You may act in that manner with those who dispute by established rules: we live from hand to mouth, and say any thing that strikes our mind with probability, so that we are only at liberty. But because I just now spoke of consistency, I do not think the inquiry in this place is, if Zeno's and his hearer Aristo's opinion be true, that nothing is good but what is honest; but, admitting that, then, whether the whole of a happy life can be rested on virtue alone. Wherefore if we certainly grant Brutus this, that a wise man is always happy, how consistent he is, is his business: for who indeed is more worthy than himself of the glory of that opinion? Still we may maintain that the same is most happy; though Zeno of Citium, a stranger and a mean coiner of words, has insinuated himself into the old philosophy.

XII. Yet the prevalence of this opinion is due to the

authority of Plato, who often makes use of this expression, "that nothing but virtue can be entitled to the name of good:" agreeably to what Socrates saith in Plato's Gorgias, when one asked him, if he did not think Archelaus the son of Perdiccas, who was then looked on as the most fortunate person, a very happy man? "I do not know," replied he, "for I never conversed with him. What, is there no other way you can know it by? None at all. You cannot then pronounce of the great king of the Persians, whether he is happy or not? How can I, when I do not know how learned or how good a man he is? What! Do you look on a happy life to depend on that? My opinion entirely is, that good men are happy, and the wicked miserable. Is Archelaus then miserable? Certainly, if unjust." Now doth it not appear to you, that he placed the whole of a happy life in virtue alone? But what doth the same say in his funeral oration? "For," saith he, "whoever has every thing that relates to a happy life so compact within himself, as not to be connected with the good or bad fortune of another, and not to depend on what befalls another, or be under any uncertainty, such a one has acquired the best rule of living: this is that moderate, that brave, that wise man, who submits to the gain and loss of every thing, and especially of his children, and obeys that old precept; so as never to be too joyful or too sad, because he depends entirely upon himself."

XIII. From Plato therefore all my discourse shall be deduced, as it were, from some sacred and hallowed fountain. Whence can I then more properly begin, than from nature, the parent of all? For whatsoever she produces, not only of the animal sort, but even of the vegetable, she designed it to be perfect in its respective kind. So that among trees, and vines, and those lower plants and trees, which cannot advance themselves higher from the earth, some are ever green; others are stripped of their leaves in winter, and, warmed by the spring season, put them out afresh; and there are none of them but what are so quickened by a certain interior motion, and their own seeds inclosed in every one, so as to yield flowers, fruit, or berries, that all may have every perfection that belongs to it, provided no violence prevents it. But the force of nature itself may be more easily discovered in animals, as she has bestowed sense on them. For those animals that can swim she designed inhabitants of the water; those that fly, to expatiate in the air; some creeping, some walking: of these very animals some are solitary, some herding together; some wild, others tame, some hidden and covered by the earth; and every one of these maintains the law of nature, confining itself to what was bestowed on it, and unable to change its manner of life. And as every animal has from nature something that distinguishes it, which every one maintains and never quits; so man has something far more excellent, though every thing is said to excel by comparison. But the human mind, as derived from the divine reason, can be compared with nothing but with the Deity itself, if I may be allowed the expression. This then, when improved, and its perception so preserved, as not to be blinded by errors, becomes a perfect understanding, that is, absolute reason: which is the very same as virtue. And if every thing is happy which wants nothing, and is complete and perfect in its kind, and that is the peculiar lot of virtue; certainly all who are possessed of virtue are happy. And in this I agree with Brutus, even with Aristotle, Xenocrates, Speusippus, Polemon. To me such only appear completely happy: for what can he want to a complete happy life, who relies on his own good qualities, or how can he be happy who doth not rely on them?

XIV. But he who makes a threefold division of goods, must necessarily be diffident; for how can he depend on having a sound body, or that his fortune shall continue? but no one can be happy without an immovable, fixed, and permanent good. What then is this opinion of theirs? So that I think that saying of the Spartan may be applied to them, who, on some merchant's boasting before him, that he could despatch ships to every maritime coast, replied, that a fortune which depended on ropes was not very desirable. Can there be any doubt that whatever may be lost, cannot be of the number of those things which complete a happy life? for of all that constitutes a happy life, nothing will admit of growing old, of wearing out or decaying; for whoever is apprehensive of any loss in these cannot be happy: the happy man should be safe, well fenced, well fortified, out of the reach of all annoyance; not under trifling apprehensions, but void of all. As he is not called innocent who but slightly offends, but who offends not at all: so is he only to be held without fear, not who is in but little fear, but who is void of all fear. For what else is courage but an affection of mind, that is ready to undergo perils, as well as to bear pain and labour without any allay of fear? Now this certainly could not be the case, if any thing were good but what depended on honesty alone. But how can any one be in possession of that desirable and much requested security (for I now call a freedom from anxiety a security, on which freedom a happy life depends) who has, or may have, a multitude of evils attending him? How can he be brave and undaunted, and hold every thing as trifles which can befall a man, for so a wise man should do, but who thinks every thing depends on himself? Could the Lacedæmonians without this, when Philip threatened to prevent all their attempts, have asked him, if he could prevent their killing themselves? Is it not easier then to find a man of such a spirit as we inquire after, than to meet with a whole city of such men? Now, if to this courage I am speaking of, we add temperance, that governs all our commotions, what can be wanting to complete his happiness who is secured by his courage from uneasiness and fear; and is prevented from immoderate desires, and immoderate insolence of joy, by temperance? I could shew virtue able to effect these, but that I have explained on the foregoing days.

XV. But as the perturbations of the mind make life miserable, and tranquillity renders it happy: and as these perturbations are of two sorts; grief and fear, proceeding from imagined evils, immoderate joy and lust, from the mistake of what is good; and all these are in opposition to reason and counsel; when you see a man at ease, quite free and disengaged from such troublesome commotions, which are so much at variance with one another, can you hesitate to pronounce such a one a happy man? Now the wise man is always in such a disposition: therefore the wise man is always happy. Besides, every good is pleasant; whatever is pleasant may be boasted and talked of; whatever is so, is glorious; but whatever is glorious is certainly laudable, whatever is laudable doubtless, too, honest; whatever then is good, is honest. But what they reckon good, they themselves do not call honest: therefore what is honest alone is good. Hence it follows that a happy life is comprised in honesty alone. Such things then are not to be called or held for goods, amidst the abundance of which a man may be most miserable. Is there any doubt but that one who enjoys the best health, has strength, beauty, has his senses in their utmost quickness and perfection; suppose him likewise, if you please, nimble and alert, nay, give him riches, honours, authority, power, glory; now, I say, should this person, who is in possession of all these, be unjust, intemperate, timid, stupid, or an ideot; could you hesitate to call such a one miserable? What then are those goods, in the possessing which you may be very miserable? Let us see then if a happy life is not made up of parts of the same nature, as a heap implies a quantity of grain of the same kind. Which admitted, happiness must be compounded of goods, which alone are honest; if there is any mixture of things of another sort with these, nothing honest can proceed from such a composition: now, take away honesty, how can you imagine any thing happy? For whatever is good is desirable on that account: whatever is desirable must certainly be approved of: whatever you approve of must be looked on as acceptable and welcome. You must consequently assign dignity to this; and if so, it must necessarily be laudable; therefore every thing that is laudable, is good. Hence it follows, that honesty is the only good. Should we not look on it in this light, we must call a great many things good.

XVI. Not to mention riches, which, as any one, let him be ever so unworthy, may have them, I do not reckon amongst goods, for good is not attainable by all. I pass over notoriety, and popular fame, raised by the united voice of knaves and fools: even things which are absolute nothings, may be called goods; as white teeth, handsome eyes, a good complexion, and what was commended by Euryclea when she was washing Ulysses's feet, the softness of his skin, and the mildness of his discourse. If you look on these as goods, what greater encomiums can the gravity of a philosopher be entitled to, than the wild opinion of the vulgar, and the thoughtless crowd? The Stoics give the name of excellent and choice to what the others call good: they call them so indeed; but they do not allow them to complete a happy life: but these think there is no life happy without them; or, admitting it to be happy, they deny it to be the most happy. But our opinion is, that it is the most happy: and we prove it from that conclusion of Socrates. For thus that author of philosophy argued: that as the disposition of a man's mind is, so is the man: such as the man is, such will be his discourse: his actions will correspond with his discourse, and his life with his actions. But the disposition of a good man's mind is laudable, the life therefore of a good man is laudable: it is honest therefore, because laudable; the inference from which is, that the life of good men is happy. For, good gods! did I not make it appear, by my former disputations,—or was I only amusing myself and killing time, in what I then said,—that the mind of a wise man was always free from every hasty motion, which I call a perturbation? A temperate man then, constant, without fear or grief, without any immoderate joy or desire, cannot be otherwise than happy; but a wise man is always so; therefore always happy. Why then cannot a good man make every thing he thinks, or doth, regard what is laudable? For he has respect in every thing to living happily: a happy life then is laudable; but nothing is laudable without virtue; a happy life then is the effect of virtue.

XVII. The inference is made too in this manner. A wicked life has nothing to be spoken of nor gloried in: nor has that life, which is neither happy nor miserable. But there is a kind of life that admits of being spoken of and gloried in, and boasted of, as Epaminondas saith,

> The wings of Sparta's pride my counsels clipt.

Thus Africanus:

> Who, from beyond Mæotis, to the place
> Where the sun rises, deeds like mine can trace?

If then there is such a thing as a happy life, it is to be gloried in, spoken of, and commended by the person who enjoys it; but there is nothing, excepting that, which can be spoken of, or gloried in; which admitted, you know what follows. Now unless an honourable life is a happy life, there must of course be something preferable to a happy life. For they will certainly grant honour to have the preference. Thus there will be something better than a happy life: than which what can be more absurd? What! When they grant vice to be effectual to the rendering life miserable, must they not admit the same force to be in virtue to the making it happy? For contraries follow from contraries. And here I ask, what they think of Critolaus's balance? who, having put the goods of the mind into one scale, and the goods of the body and other external advantages into the other, thought the goods of the mind so to outweigh them, as to outbalance even the earth and sea.

XVIII. What hinders then that gravest of philosophers, and Xenocrates too, who raises virtue so high, and who lessens and depreciates every thing else, from not only placing a happy life, but the happiest, in virtue? which were it not so, virtue would be absolutely lost. For whoever is subject to grief, must necessarily be subject to fear too; for fear is an uneasy apprehension of future grief: and whoever is subject to fear, is liable to dread, timidity, consternation, cowardice. Therefore such a one may some time or other be over forward, nor think himself concerned with that precept of Atreus,

Through his whole life a stranger to defeat.

But such a one as I said will be defeated, and not only defeated, but made a slave of. But we would have virtue always free, always invincible: and were it not so, there would be an end of virtue. But if virtue hath in herself all that is necessary for a good life, she is certainly sufficient for happiness: virtue is certainly sufficient too for our living with courage; if with courage, then with a great mind, and indeed so as never to be under any fear, and thus to be always invincible. Hence it follows, that there can be nothing to be repented of, no wants, no lets or hinderances. Thus all things must be prosperous, perfect, and as you would have them; and consequently happy; but virtue is sufficient for living with courage, and therefore able to make your life happy. For as folly, even when possessed of what it desires, never thinks it has acquired enough: so wisdom is always satisfied with the present, and never repents on her own account. Look but on the single consulate of Lælius, and that too after having been set aside (though when a wise and good man, like him, is outvoted, the people are disappointed of a good consul, rather than he disappointed by a vain people); but the point is, would you prefer, were it in your power, to be once such a consul as Lælius, or be elected four times as Cinna? I am very well satisfied what answer you will make, and it is on that account I put the question to you.

XIX. I will not ask every one this question; for some one perhaps might answer, that he would not only prefer four consulates to one, but even one day of Cinna's life, to ages of many and famous men. Lælius would have suffered, had he but touched any one with his finger; but Cinna ordered the head of his colleague consul Cn. Octavius to be struck off; and of P. Crassus and L. Cæsar, those excellent men, so renowned both at home and abroad. Even M. Antonius, the greatest orator I ever heard; with C. Cæsar, who seems to me to have been the pattern of humanity, politeness, sweetness of temper, and wit. Could he then be happy who occasioned the death of these? So far from it, that he not only seems to me miserable for doing thus, but for acting in such a manner, that it was even lawful for him to do it, though it is unlawful for any one to do wicked actions; but this proceeds from inaccuracy of speech, for we call whatever a man is allowed to do, lawful. Was not Marius happier, I pray you, when he shared the glory of the victory gained over the Cimbrians, with his colleague Catulus, who was almost another Lælius, (for I look upon him as very like,) than, when conqueror in the civil war, he in a passion answered the friends of Catulus, who were interceding for him, "Let him die," and this he did not once, but often? In which he was happier who submitted to that barbarous decree, than he who issued it. And it is better to receive an injury than to do one; so was it better to advance a little to meet that death, that was making its approaches, as Catulus did, than, like Marius, to sully the glory of six consulates, and disgrace his latter days by the death of such a man.

XX. Dionysius exercised his tyranny over the Syracusians thirty-eight years, being but twenty-five years old when he seized on the government. How beautiful and how wealthy a city did he oppress with slavery! And yet we have it from good authority, that he was remarkably temperate in his manner of living, that he was very quick and diligent in carrying on business, but naturally mischievous and unjust. Whence every one who diligently inquires into truth, must necessarily see that he was very miserable. Neither did he attain what he so greatly desired, even when he was persuaded he had unlimited power. For notwithstanding he was of a good family and reputable parents, (though that is contested,) and had a great acquaintance of intimate friends and relations, he could not trust any one of them, but committed the guard of his person to some slaves, whom he had selected from rich men's families and made free, and to strangers and barbarians. And thus, through an unjust desire of governing, he in a manner shut himself up in a prison. Besides, he would not trust his throat to a barber, but had his daughters taught to shave; so that these royal virgins were forced to descend to the base and slavish employment of shaving the head and beard of their father. Nor would he trust even them, when they were grown up, with a razor: but contrived how they might burn off the hair of his head and beard with red-hot nutshells. And as to his two wives, Aristomache his countrywoman, and Doris of Locris, he never visited them at night before every thing had been well searched and examined. And as he had surrounded the place where his bed was with a broad ditch, and made a way over it with a wooden bridge; he drew that bridge over, after shutting his bedchamber door. And as he did not dare to stand where they usually harangued, he generally addressed the people from a high tower. And it is said, that when he was disposed to play at tennis, for he delighted much in it, and had pulled off his clothes, he used to give his sword into the keeping of a young man whom he was very fond of. On this one of his intimates said pleasantly, "You certainly trust your life with him:" the young man happening to smile at this, he ordered them both to be slain; the one for shewing how he might be taken off, the other for approving of what was said by his smiling. But he was so concerned at what he had done, that nothing affected him more during his whole life: for he had slain one he was extremely partial to. Thus do weak men's desires pull them different ways, and whilst they indulge one, they act counter to another. This tyrant, however, shewed how happy he esteemed himself.

XXI. For whilst Damocles, one of his flatterers, was talking in conversation about his forces, his wealth, the greatness of his power, the plenty he enjoyed, the grandeur of his royal palaces, and was maintaining that no one was ever happier; "Have you an inclination," saith he, "Damocles, as this kind of life pleases you, to have a taste of it yourself, and try to make a trial of the good fortune that attends me?" "I should be glad to make the experiment," says Damocles: upon which Dionysius ordered him to be laid on a bed of gold, with the most beautiful covering, embroidered, and wrought in a high taste, and he dressed out a great many sideboards with silver and embossed gold. He then ordered some youths, distinguished for their handsome persons, to wait at his table, and to observe his nod, in order to serve him with what he wanted. There were ointments and garlands; perfumes were burned; tables provided with the most exquisite meats. Damocles thought himself very happy. In the midst of this apparatus Dionysius ordered a bright sword to be let down from the ceiling, tied by a horsehair, so as to hang over the head of that happy man. After which he neither cast his eye on those handsome waiters, nor on the well-wrought plate; nor touched any of the provisions; the garlands fell to pieces. At last he entreated the tyrant to give him leave to go, for that now he had no desire to be happy. Doth not Dionysius, then, seem to have declared there can be no happiness with one who is under constant apprehensions? But he was not now at liberty to return to justice, and restore his citizens their rights and privileges; for by the indiscretion of youth he had engaged in so many wrong steps, and committed such extravagancies, that had he attempted to have returned to a right way of thinking, he must have endangered his life.

XXII. Yet how desirous he was of those very friends whose fidelity he dreaded, appears from the two Pythagoreans: one of these had been security for his friend, who was condemned to die; the other, to release his security, presented himself at the time appointed for his dying: "I wish," said Dionysius, "you would admit me as a third." What misery was it for him to be deprived of acquaintance, of company at his table, and of the freedom of conversation; especially for one who was a man of learning, and from his childhood acquainted with liberal arts, very fond of music, and himself a tragedian; how good a one is not to the purpose, for I know not how it is, but in this way, more than any other, every one thinks his own performances excellent; I never as yet knew any poet (and Aquinius was my friend) who did not give himself the preference. The case is this, you are pleased with your own, I like mine. But to return to Dionysius: he debarred himself from all civil and polite conversation, spent his life among fugitives, bondmen, and barbarians: for he was persuaded no one could be his friend, who was worthy of liberty, or had the least desire of being free. Shall I not then prefer the life of Plato and Archytas, manifestly wise and learned men, to his, than which nothing can possibly be more horrid and miserable?

XXIII. I will present you with an humble and obscure mathematician of the same city, called Archimedes, who lived many years after; whose tomb, overgrown with shrubs and briars, I in my quæstorship discovered, when the Syracusians knew nothing of it, and even denied that there was any such thing remaining: for I remembered some verses, which I had been informed were engraved on his monument. These set forth, that on the top of it there was placed a sphere with a cylinder. When I had carefully examined all the monuments (for there are a great many) at the gate Achradinæ, I observed a small column standing out a little above the briars, with the figure of a sphere and a cylinder upon it; whereupon I immediately said to the Syracusians, for there were some of their principal magistrates there, that I imagined that was what I was inquiring for. Several men being sent in with scythes, cleared the way, and made an opening for us. When we could get at it, and were come near to the front base of it, I found the inscription, though the latter parts of all the verses were effaced almost half away. Thus one of the noblest cities of Greece, and once, likewise, the most learned, had known nothing of the monument of its most ingenious citizen, if it had not been discovered to them by a native of Arpinum. But to return from whence I have rambled. Who is there in the least acquainted with the Muses, that is, with liberal knowledge, or that deals at all in learning, who would not choose to be this mathematician rather than that tyrant? If we look into their methods of living and their employments, we shall find the mind of the one strengthened and improved, with tracing the deductions of reason, amused with his own ingenuity, the sweetest food of the mind; the thoughts of the other engaged in continual murders and injuries, in constant fears by night and by day. Now imagine a Democritus, a Pythagoras, and an Anaxagoras; what kingdom, what riches, would you prefer to their studies and amusements? for you must necessarily look there for the best of every thing, where the excellency of man is; but what is there better in man than a sagacious and good mind? Now the enjoying of that good can alone make us happy: but virtue is the good of the mind; it follows, therefore, that a happy life depends on that. Hence proceed all things that are beautiful, honest, and excellent, as I said above: but these, I think, must be treated of more at large, for they are well stored with joys. For as it is clear that a happy life consists in perpetual and unexhausted pleasures, it follows too that a happy life must arise from honesty.

XXIV. But that what I propose to demonstrate to you may not rest in mere words only, I must set before you the picture of something, as it were, living and moving in the world, that may dispose us more for the improvement of the understanding and real knowledge. Let us then pitch upon some man perfectly acquainted with the most excellent arts; let us present him for a while to our own thoughts, and figure him to our own imaginations. In the first place, he must necessarily be of an extraordinary capacity; for virtue is not easily connected with dull minds. Next, he must have a great desire of discovering truth, from whence will arise that threefold production of the mind: one depends on knowing things, and explaining nature; the other in defining what we should desire, and what avoid; the third in judging of consequences and impossibilities: in which consists as well subtilty in disputing, as clearness of judgment. Now with what pleasure must the mind of a wise man be affected, which continually dwells in the midst of such cares and engagements as these, when he views the revolutions and motions of the whole world, and sees those innumerable stars in the heavens, which, though fixed in their places, yet have a common motion with the whole; and observes the seven other stars, some higher, some lower, each maintaining their own course, while their motions, though wandering, have limited and appointed spaces to run through! The sight of which doubtless urged and encouraged those ancient philosophers to employ their search on many other things. Hence arose an inquiry after the beginnings, and, as it were, seeds from whence all things were produced and composed; what was the origin of every kind, as well animate as inanimate, articulate as inarticulate; what occasioned their beginning and end, and by what alteration and change one thing was converted into another: whence the earth, and by what weights it was balanced: by what caverns the seas were supplied: by what gravity all things being carried down tend always to the middle of the world, which in any round body is the lowest place.

XXV. A mind employed on such subjects, and which night and day contemplates on them, has in itself that precept of the Delphic god, to "know itself," and to perceive its connexion with the divine reason, from whence it is filled with an insatiable joy. For reflections on the power and nature of the gods raise a desire of imitating their eternity. Nor doth the mind, that sees the necessary dependencies and connexions that one cause has with another, think itself confinable to the shortness of this life. Those causes, though they proceed from eternity to eternity, are governed by reason and understanding. Whoever beholds these and examines them, or rather whose view takes in all the parts and boundaries of things, with what tranquillity of mind doth he look on all human affairs, and what is nearer him! Hence proceeds the knowledge of virtue; hence arise the kinds and species of virtues; hence is discovered what nature regards as the bounds and extremities of good and evil, to what all duties have respect, and which is the most eligible manner of life. One great effect that arises from informing himself of these, and such like things, is, that virtue is of itself sufficient to a happy life; which is the subject of this disputation.

The third qualification of our wise man comes next, which goes through and spreads itself over every part of wisdom; it is that whereby we define every particular thing, distinguish the genus from its species, connect consequences, draw just conclusions, and distinguish true and false, which is the very art and science of disputing; which is not only of the greatest use in the examination of what passes in the world, but is likewise the most rational entertainment, and most becoming true wisdom. Such are its effects in retirement. Now let our wise man be considered as protecting the republic; what can be more excellent than such a character? By his prudence he will discover the true interests of his fellow-citizens, by his justice he will be prevented from applying what belongs to the public to his own use; and, in short, he will be ever governed by all the virtues, which are many and various. To these let us add the advantage of his friendships; in which the learned reckon not only a natural harmony and agreement of sentiments throughout the conduct of life, but the utmost pleasure and satisfaction in conversing and passing our time constantly with one another. What can be wanting to such a life as this, to make it more happy than it is? Fortune herself must yield to a life stored with such joys. Now if it be a happiness to rejoice in such goods of the mind, that is, virtue, and all wise men enjoy thoroughly these pleasures; it must necessarily be granted, that all such are happy.

XXVI. *A.* What, when in torments and on the rack? *M.* Do you imagine I am speaking of him as laid on roses and violets? Is it allowable even for Epicurus (who only affects being a philosopher, and who assumed that name to himself) to say, and, as matters stand, I commend him for his saying, a wise man may at all times cry out, though he be burned, tortured, cut to pieces, How little I regard it? Shall this be said by one who defines all evil by pain, every good by pleasure; who could ridicule whatever we say either of what is honest, or what is base, and could declare of us that we were employed about words, and discharging mere empty sounds; and that nothing is to be regarded, but as it is perceived smooth or rough by the body? What, shall such a man as this, as I said, whose understanding is little superior to the beasts, be at liberty to forget himself; and not only despise fortune, when the whole of his good and evil is in the power of fortune, but say, that he is happy in the most racking torture, when he had actually declared pain not only the greatest evil, but the only one? And all this without having recourse to our remedies for bearing pain, such as firmness of mind, a shame of doing any thing base, exercise, and the habit of patience, precepts of courage, and a manly hardiness: but saith, he supports himself on the single recollection of past pleasure; as if any one, being so hot as scarce to be able to bear it, should attempt to recollect that he was once in my country Arpinum, where he was surrounded on every side by cooling streams; for I do not apprehend how past pleasures can allay present evils. But when he saith that a wise man is always happy, who has no right to say so, can he be consistent with himself? What may they not do, who allow nothing to be desirable, nothing to be looked on as good, but what is honest? Let then the Peripatetics and old Academics follow my example, and at length leave off to mutter to themselves: and openly, and with a clear voice, let them be bold to say, that a happy life may descend into Phalaris's bull.

XXVII. But to dismiss the subtilties of the Stoics, which I am sensible I have dealt more in than necessary, let us admit of three kinds of goods: let them really be the three kinds of goods, provided no regard is had to the body, and externals, as no otherwise entitled to the appellation of good, than as we are obliged to use them: but let those other and divine goods spread themselves far and near, and reach the very heavens. Why then may I not call him happy, nay, the happiest, who has attained them? Shall a wise man be afraid of pain? which is, indeed, the greatest enemy to our opinion. For I am persuaded we are prepared and fortified sufficiently, by the disputations of the foregoing days, against our own death, or the death of our friends, against grief and the other perturbations of the mind. Pain seems to be the sharpest adversary of virtue, that threatens us with burning torches; that threatens to take down our fortitude, greatness of mind, and patience. Shall virtue then yield to this? Shall the happy life of a wise and constant man submit to this? Good gods! how base would this be! Spartan boys will bear to have their bodies torn by rods, without uttering a groan. I myself saw, at Lacedæmon, troops of young men, with great earnestness contending together with their hands and feet, with their teeth and nails, nay, even ready to expire, rather than own themselves conquered. Is any country more savagely barbarous than India? Yet they have amongst them some that are held for wise men, who never wear any clothes all their life long, and bear the snow of Caucasus, and the piercing cold of winter, without any pain; and will throw themselves into the fire to be burned without a groan. The women too in India, on the death of their husbands, apply to the judge to have it determined which of them was best beloved by him: for it is customary there for one man to have many wives. She in whose favour it is determined, attended by her relations, is laid on the pile with her husband: the others, who are postponed, walk away very much dejected. Custom can never be superior to nature: for nature is never to be got the better of. But our minds are infected by sloth and idleness, delicacies, languor, and indolence: we have enervated them by opinions, and bad customs. Who but knows the manner of the Egyptians? Their minds being tainted by pernicious opinions, they are ready to bear any torture, rather than hurt an ibis, a snake, cat, dog, or crocodile: and should any one inadvertently have hurt any of these, they submit to any punishment. So far of human nature. As to the beasts, do they not bear cold, hunger, running about in woods, and on mountains and deserts? Will they not fight for their young ones till they are wounded? Are they afraid of any attacks or blows? I mention not what the ambitious will suffer for honour's sake, or those who are desirous of praise on account of glory, or lovers to gratify their lust. Life is full of such instances.

XXVIII. But not to dwell too much on these, and to return to our purpose. I say, and say again, that happiness will submit even to be tormented; and after having accompanied justice, temperance, but principally fortitude, greatness of soul and patience will not stop short at sight of the executioner; and when all other virtues proceed calmly to the torture, will that halt, as I said, on the outside and threshold of the prison? for what can be baser, what can carry a worse appearance, than to be left alone, separated from those beautiful attendants? which can by no means be the case: for neither can the virtues hold together without happiness, nor happiness without the virtues: so that they will not suffer her to desert them, but will carry that along with them, to whatever torments, to whatever pain they are led. For it is the peculiar quality of a wise man to do nothing that he may repent of, nothing against his inclination: but always to act nobly, with constancy, gravity, and honesty: to depend on nothing as certain: to wonder at nothing, when it falls out, as if it appeared new and unexpected to him: to be independent of every one, and abide by his own opinion. For my part, I cannot form an idea of any thing happier than this. The conclusion of the Stoics indeed is easy, as they are persuaded that the end of good is to live agreeably to nature, and be consistent with that; as a wise man should do so, not only because it is his duty, but because it is in his power. It must of course follow, that whoever has the chief good in his power, has his happiness so too. Thus the life of a wise man is always happy. You have here what I think may be confidently said of a happy life, and as things are now, very truly, unless you can advance something better.

XXIX. *A.* Indeed I cannot; but I would willingly request of you, unless it is troublesome, (as you are under no confinement from obligations to any particular sect, but gather from all of them whatever most strikes you with the appearance of probability,) as you just now seemed to advise the Peripatetics, and the old Academy, boldly to speak out without reserve, "that wise men are always the happiest," I should be glad to hear how you think it consistent for them to say so, when you have said so much against that opinion, and the conclusions of the Stoics. *M.* I will make use then of that liberty, which none but ourselves have the privilege of using in philosophy, whose discourses determine nothing, but take in every thing, leaving them, unsupported by any authority, to be judged of by others, according to their weight. And as you seem desirous of knowing why, notwithstanding the different opinion of philosophers, with regard to the ends of goods, virtue may have sufficient security for a happy life: which security, as we are informed, Carneades used indeed to dispute against: but he disputed as against the Stoics, whose opinions he combated with great zeal and vehemence; but I shall handle it with more temper: for if the Stoics have rightly settled the *ends* of goods, the affair is at an end; for a wise man must necessarily be always happy. But let us examine, if we can, the particular opinions of the others, that this excellent decision, if I may so call it, of a happy life, may be agreeable to the opinions and discipline of all.

XXX. These then are the opinions, as I think, that are held and defended: the first four simple ones; "that nothing is good but what is honest," according to the Stoics: "nothing good but pleasure," as Epicurus maintains: "nothing good but a freedom from pain," as Hieronymus asserts: "nothing good but an enjoyment of the principal, or all, or the greatest goods of nature," as Carneades maintained against the Stoics:

these are simple, the others mixed. Three kinds of goods: the greatest those of the mind, the next those of the body. The third were external goods, as the Peripatetics say, and the old Academics differ very little from them. Clitomachus and Callipho have coupled pleasure with honesty: but Diodorus, the Peripatetic, has joined indolence to honesty. These are the opinions that have some footing; for those of Aristo, Pyrrho, Herillus, and of some others, are quite out of date. Now let us see what they have of weight in them, excepting the Stoics, whose opinion I think I have sufficiently defended; and indeed I have explained what the Peripatetics have to say; excepting that Theophrastus, and those who followed him, dread and abhor pain in too weak a manner. The others may go on to exaggerate the gravity and dignity of virtue, as usual; which when they have extolled to the skies, with the usual extravagance of good orators, it is easy to reduce the other to nothing by comparison, and to despise them. They who think praise is to be acquired by pain, are not at liberty to deny those to be happy who have acquired it. Though they may be under some evils, yet this name of happy extends very widely.

XXXI. Even as trading is said to be lucrative, and farming advantageous, not because the one never meets with any loss, or the other no damage from the inclemency of the weather, but because they succeed in general: so life may be properly called happy, not from its being entirely made up of good things, but as it abounds with these to a great and considerable degree. By this way of reasoning, then, a happy life may attend virtue even to punishments; nay, may descend with her into Phalaris's bull, according to Aristotle, Xenocrates, Speusippus, Polemon; and will not be gained over by any allurements to forsake her. Of the same opinion will Calliphon and Diodorus be: both of them such friends to virtue, as to think all things should be discarded and far removed, that are compatible with it. The rest seem to be more scrupulous about these things, but yet get clear of them; as Epicurus, Hieronymus, and whoever thinks it worth while to defend the deserted Carneades: not one of them but thinks the mind to be judge of those goods, and can sufficiently instruct him how to despise what has the appearance only of good or evil. For what seems to you to be the case with Epicurus, it is the same with Hieronymus and Carneades, and indeed with all the rest of them: for who is not sufficiently prepared against death and pain? I will begin, with your leave, with him whom we call soft and voluptuous. What! doth he seem to you to be afraid of death or pain, who calls the day of his death happy; and when affected by the greatest pains, silences them all by recollecting arguments of his own discovering? And this is not done in such a manner as to give room for imagining that he talks thus wildly on a sudden start: but his opinion of death is, that on the dissolution of the animal, all sense is lost; and what is deprived of sense, as he thinks, can no way affect us. And as to pain, he has his maxims too: if great, the comfort is, that it must be short; if of long continuance, it must be tolerable. What then? Do those great boasters declare any thing better than Epicurus, in opposition to these two things which distress us the most? And as to other things, do not Epicurus and the rest of the philosophers seem sufficiently prepared? Who doth not dread poverty? And yet no true philosopher ever can.

XXXII. But with how little is this man satisfied?

No one has said more on frugality. For when a man is far removed from those things which occasion a desire of money, from love, ambition, or other daily expenses; why should he be fond of money, or concern himself at all about it? Could the Scythian Anacharsis disregard money, and shall not our philosophers be able to do so? We are informed of an epistle of his, in these words: "Anacharsis to Hanno, greeting. My clothing is as the Scythians cover themselves; the hardness of my feet supplies the want of shoes; the ground is my bed, hunger my sauce, my food milk, cheese, and flesh. So you may come to a man in no want. But as to those presents you take so much pleasure in, you may dispose of them to your own citizens, or to the immortal gods." Almost all the philosophers, whatever their discipline be, excepting those who are warped from right reason by a vicious disposition, are of this very opinion. Socrates, when he saw in a procession a great deal of gold and silver, cried out, "How many things are there I do not want!" Xenocrates, when some ambassadors from Alexander had brought him fifty talents, the largest money of those times, especially at Athens, carried the ambassadors to sup in the academy, and placed just a sufficiency before them, without any apparatus. When they asked him the next day, to whom he would order the money to be told out: "What?" saith he, "did you not perceive by our slight repast of yesterday, that I had no occasion for money?" But when he perceived that they were somewhat dejected, he accepted of thirty minæ, that he might not seem to disrespect the king's generosity. But Diogenes took a greater liberty as a Cynic, when Alexander asked him if he wanted any thing: "A little from the sun," said he; for Alexander hindered him from sunning himself.

And indeed this very man used to maintain how much he excelled the Persian king, in his manner of life and fortune: that he himself was in want of nothing, the other never had enough: that he had no inclination for those pleasures which could never satisfy the other; and that the other could never obtain his.

XXXIII. You see, I imagine, how Epicurus has divided his kinds of desires, not very subtilely perhaps, but usefully: that they are "partly natural and necessary; partly natural, but not necessary; partly neither." Those which are necessary may be supplied almost for nothing; for the things that nature requires are easily obtained. As to the second kind of desires, his opinion is, that any one may easily either enjoy or go without them. With regard to the third, being frivolous, as neither allied to necessity nor nature, he thinks they should be entirely rooted out. On this topic the Epicureans dispute much; and those pleasures which they do not despise, on account of their species, they reduce one by one, and seem rather for lessening the number of them: for as to wanton pleasures, of which they say a great deal, these, say they, are easy, common, and within any one's reach; and think that if nature requires them, they are not to be estimated by birth, condition, or rank, but by shape, age, and person: and that it is by no means difficult to refrain from them, should health, duty, or reputation require it; and that this kind of pleasure may be desirable, where it is attended with no inconvenience, but can never be of any use. And what he declares upon the whole of pleasure is such as shews his opinion to be, that pleasure is always desirable, to be pursued merely as a pleasure; and for the same reason pain is to be avoided, because it is pain. So that a wise man will always do himself the justice to avoid pleasure, should pain ensue from it in a greater proportion; and will submit to pain, the effects of which will be a greater pleasure: so that all pleasurable things, though the corporeal senses are the judges of them, are to be referred to the mind, on which account the body rejoices, whilst it perceives a present pleasure; but that the mind not only perceives the present as well as the body, but foresees it, whilst it is coming, and, even when it is past, will not let it quite slip away. So that a wise man enjoys a continual series of pleasures, uniting the expectation of future pleasure to the recollection of what he has already tasted. The like notions are applied by them to high living; and the magnificence and expensiveness of entertainments are deprecated, because nature is satisfied at a small expense.

XXXIV. For who doth not see this, that an appetite is the best sauce? When Darius, flying from the enemy, had drunk some water which was muddy, and tainted with dead bodies, he declared that he had never drunk any thing more pleasant; the case was, he had never drunk before when he was thirsty. Nor had Ptolemy ever ate when he was hungry: for as he was travelling over Egypt, his company not keeping up with him, he had some coarse bread presented him in a cottage: upon which he said, "Nothing ever seemed to him pleasanter than that bread." They relate of Socrates, that once walking very fast till the evening, on his being asked why he did so, his reply was, that he was purchasing an appetite by walking, that he might sup the better. And do we not see what the Lacedæmonians provide in their Phiditia? where the tyrant Dionysius supped, but told them he did not at all like that black broth, which was their principal dish; on this he who dressed it said, "It was no wonder, for it wanted seasoning." Dionysius asked what that seasoning was; to which it was replied, fatigue in hunting, sweating, a race on the banks of Eurotas, hunger, and thirst:" for these are the seasonings to the Lacedæmonian banquets. And this may not only be conceived from the custom of men, but from the beasts, who are satisfied with any thing that is thrown before them, provided it is not unnatural, and they seek no further. Some entire cities, taught by custom, are delighted with parsimony, as I said but just now of the Lacedæmonians. Xenophon has given an account of the Persian diet; who never, as he saith, use any thing but cresses with their bread, not but that, should nature require any thing more agreeable, many things might be easily supplied by the ground, and plants in great abundance, and of incomparable sweetness. Add to this, strength and health, as the consequence of this abstemious way of living. Now compare with this those who sweat and belch, crammed with eating like fatted oxen; then will you perceive that they who pursue pleasure most, attain it least; and that the pleasure of eating lies not in satiety, but appetite.

XXXV. They report of Timotheus, a famous man at Athens, and the head of the city, that having supped with Plato, and being extremely delighted with his entertainment, on seeing him the next day he said, "Your suppers are not only agreeable whilst I partake of them, but the next day also." Besides, the understanding is impaired when we are full with over-eating and drinking. There is an excellent epistle of Plato to Dion's relations. It is written almost in these words: "When I came there, that happy life so much talked of, crowded with Italian and Syracusan entertainments, was no ways agreeable to me; to be crammed twice a day, and never to have the night to yourself, and other things which attend on this kind of life, by which a man will never be made the wiser, and may be much less moderate; for it must be an extraordinary disposition that can be temperate in such circumstances." How then can a life be pleasant without prudence and moderation? Hence you discover the mistake of Sardanapalus, the wealthiest king of the Assyrians, who ordered it to be engraved on his tomb,

> I still possess what luxury did cost;
> But what I left, though excellent, is lost.

"What but this," saith Aristotle, "could be inscribed on the tomb, not of a king but an ox?" He said that he possessed those things when dead, which, in his lifetime, he could have no longer than whilst he was enjoying them. Why then are riches desired? and wherein doth poverty prevent us from being happy? In the want, I imagine, of statues, pictures, and diversions. Should any one be delighted with these, have not the poor people the enjoyment of these more than they who have them in the greatest abundance? For we have great numbers of them shewn publicly in our city. And whatever private people may have of them, they have not many of them, and they but seldom see them, only when they go to their country seats; and some of them must be stung to the heart when they consider how they came by them. The day would fail me, should I be inclined to defend the cause of poverty: the thing is manifest, and nature daily informs us, how few little trifling things she really stands in need of.

XXXVI. Let us inquire, then, if obscurity, the want of power, or even the being unpopular, can prevent a wise man from being happy? Observe if popular favour, and this glory which they are so fond of, be not attended with more uneasiness than pleasure? Our Demosthenes was certainly very weak in declaring himself pleased with a woman who carried water, as is the custom in Greece, whispering to another, "that is he, that is Demosthenes." What could be weaker than this? And yet what an orator he was! But although he had learned to speak to others, he had conversed but little with himself. We may perceive that popular glory is not desirable of itself; nor is obscurity to be dreaded. "I came to Athens," saith Democritus, "and there was no one there that knew me:" this was a moderate and grave man, who could glory in his obscurity. Shall musicians compose their tunes to their own taste? and shall a philosopher, master of a much better art, inquire not after what is most true, but what will please the people? Can any thing be more absurd than to despise the vulgar as mere unpolished mechanics, when single, and to think them of consequence when collected into a body? These wise men would contemn our ambitious pursuits, and our vanities, and would reject all honours the people could voluntarily offer to them: but we know not how to despise them, till we begin to repent of having accepted them. Heraclitus, the natural philosopher, relates thus of Hermodorus, the chief of the Ephesians: "that all the Ephesians," saith he, "ought to be punished with death, for saying, when they had expelled Hermodorus out of their city, that they would have no one amongst them better than another; if there were any such, let him go elsewhere to some other people." Is not this the case with the people every where? do they not hate every virtue that distinguishes itself? What? was not Aristides (I had rather instance in the Greeks than ourselves) banished his country for being eminently just? What troubles, then, are they free from, who have no connexions with the people! What is more agreeable than a learned retirement? I speak of that learning which makes us acquainted with the boundless extent of nature, and the universe, and in this world discovers to us both heaven, earth, and sea.

XXXVII. If then honour and riches have no value, what is there else to be afraid of? Banishment, I suppose; which is looked on as the greatest evil. Now, if the evil of banishment proceeds not from ourselves, but from the froward disposition of the people, I have just now declared how contemptible it is. But if to leave one's country be miserable, the provinces are full of miserable men: very few of those ever return to their country again. But exiles are amerced of their goods! What then? Has there not been enough said on bearing poverty? But with regard to banishment, if we examine the nature of things, not the ignominy of the name, how little doth it differ from constant travelling! In which some of the most famous philosophers have spent their whole life: as Xenocrates, Crantor, Arcesilas, Lacydes, Aristotle, Theophrastus, Zeno, Cleanthes, Chrysippus, Antipater, Carneades, Panætius, Clitomachus, Philo, Antiochus, Posidonius, and innumerable others; who from their first setting out never returned home again. Now what ignominy can a wise man be affected with, (for of such a one I speak,) who can be guilty of nothing to occasion it; for one who is banished for his deserts ought not to be comforted. Lastly, they can easily reconcile themselves to every accident, who make every thing that ensues from life conduce to pleasure; so that in whatever place these are supplied, there they may live happily. Thus what Teucer said may be applied to every case:

Wherever I am happy, there is my country.

Socrates, indeed, when asked where he belonged to, replied, "The world;" for he looked upon himself as a citizen and inhabitant of the whole world. How was it with T. Altibutius? Did he not follow his philosophical studies with the greatest satisfaction at Athens, although he was banished? which would not have happened to him, if he had obeyed the laws of Epicurus, and lived peaceably in the republic. In what was Epicurus happier, living in his country, than Metrodorus at Athens? Or did Plato's happiness exceed that of Xenocrates, or Polemo, or Arcesilas? Or is that city to be valued much, that banishes all her good and wise men? Demaratus, the father of our king Tarquin, not being able to bear the tyrant Cypselus, fled from Corinth to Tarquinii, settled there, and had children. How, was it an unwise act in him to prefer the liberty of banishment to slavery at home?

XXXVIII. Besides the emotions of the mind, all griefs and anxieties are assuaged by forgetting them, and turning our thoughts to pleasure. Therefore it was not without reason that Epicurus presumed to say, that a wise man abounds with good things, because he may always have his pleasures. From whence, as he thinks, our point is gained, that a wise man should be always happy. What! though he should be deprived of the senses of seeing and hearing? Yes: for he holds those things very cheap. For, in the first place, what are the pleasures we are deprived of by that dreadful thing, blindness? For though they allow other pleasures to be confined to the senses, yet what are perceived by the sight do not depend wholly on the pleasure the eyes receive; as when we taste, smell, touch, or hear; in all these, the organs themselves are the seat of pleasure; but it is not so with the eyes. The mind is entertained by what we see; but the mind may be entertained many ways, though we could not see at all. I am speaking of a learned and wise man, with whom to think is to live. But thinking with a wise man doth not altogether require the use of his eyes in his investigations; for if night doth not strip him of his happiness, why should blindness, which resembles night, have that effect? For the reply of Antipater the Cyrenaic to some women who bewailed his being blind, though it is a little too obscene, had no bad meaning. "What do you mean," saith he; "do you think the night can furnish no pleasure?" And we find by his magistracies and his actions, that old Appius too, who was blind many years, was not prevented from doing whatever was required of him, with respect to the public or his own affairs. It is said that C. Drusus's house was crowded with clients. When they, whose business it was, could not see how to conduct themselves, they applied to a blind guide.

XXXIX. When I was a boy, Cn. Aufidius, a blind man, who had served the office of prætor, not only gave his opinion in the senate, and was ready to assist his friends, but wrote a Greek history, and had an insight into literature. Diodorus the Stoic was blind, and lived many years at my house. He indeed, which is scarce credible, besides applying himself more than usual to philosophy, and playing on the flute agreeably to the custom of the Pythagoreans, and having books read to him night and day, in all which he did not want eyes, contrived to teach geometry, which one would think could hardly be done without the assistance of eyes, telling his scholars how and where to describe every line. They relate of

Asclepiades, no obscure Eretric philosopher, when one asked him what inconveniences he suffered from his blindness, that his reply was, "He was at the expense of another servant." So that, as the most extreme poverty may be borne, if you please, as is daily the case with some in Greece; so blindness may easily be borne, provided you have the proper supports of health. Democritus was so blind he could not distinguish white from black: but he knew the difference betwixt good and evil, just and unjust, honest and base, the useful and useless, great and small. Thus one may live happily without distinguishing colours; but without acquainting yourself with things, you cannot; and this man was of opinion, that the intense application of the mind was taken off by the objects that presented themselves to the eye, and while others often could not see what was before their feet, he travelled through all infinity. It is reported also that Homer was blind, but we observe his painting, as well as his poetry. What country, what coast, what part of Greece, what military attacks, what dispositions of battle, what army, what ship, what motions of men and animals, has he not so described as to make us see what he could not see himself? What, then, can we imagine Homer, or any other learned man, can want to entertain his mind? Were it not so, would Anaxagoras, or this very Democritus, have left their estates and patrimonies, and given themselves up to the pursuit of acquiring this divine entertainment? It is thus that the poets, who have represented Tiresias the Augur as a wise man, blind, never exhibit him as bewailing his blindness. But as Homer had described Polypheme as a monster and a wild man, he represents him talking with his ram, and speaking of his good fortune, that he could go wherever he pleased and touch what he would. And so far he was right, for that Cyclops was of much the same understanding with his ram.

XL. Now as to the evil of being deaf; M. Crassus was a little thick of hearing: but it was more uneasiness to him that he heard himself ill spoken of; though, in my opinion, without reason. Our Epicureans cannot understand Greek, nor the Greeks Latin; now, they are deaf reciprocally as to each other's language, and we are all truly deaf with regard to those innumerable languages which we do not understand. They do not hear the voice of the harper, but then they do not hear the grating of a saw when it is setting, or the grunting of a hog when his throat is cutting, nor the roaring of the sea when they are desirous of rest. And if they should chance to be fond of singing, they ought, in the first place, to consider that many wise men lived happily before music was discovered; besides, they may have more pleasure in reading verses, than in hearing them sung. Then, as I before referred the blind to the pleasures of hearing, so I may the deaf to the pleasures of sight: moreover, whoever can converse with himself doth not need the conversation of another. But supposing all these misfortunes to meet in one person: suppose him blind and deaf, let him be afflicted with the sharpest pains of body, which, in the first place, generally of themselves make an end of him: but should they continue so long, and the pain be so exquisite, that there should be no reason for bearing them, why, good gods, should we be under any difficulty? For there is a retreat at hand;—death is that retreat—a shelter where we shall for ever be insensible. Theodorus said to Lysimachus, who threatened him with death, "It is a great matter indeed for you to do what cantharides can." When Perses entreated Paulus not to lead him in triumph,

"That is as you please," said Paulus. I said many things of death in our first day's disputation, when death was the subject; and not a little the next day, when I treated of pain; which things if you recollect, there can be no danger of your looking upon death as undesirable, or at least it will not be dreadful.

XLI. That custom in force with the Grecians at their banquets, should, in my opinion, take place in life: Drink, say they, or leave the company; and right enough: let him either enjoy the pleasure of drinking with others, or not stay till he meets with affronts from those that are in liquor. Thus those injuries of fortune you cannot bear, you should leave. This is the very same which is said by Epicurus and Hieronymus. Now if those philosophers, whose opinion it is that virtue has no power of itself, and who say that what we denominate honest and laudable imply nothing, and are only set off with an unmeaning sound; can they nevertheless maintain that a wise man is always happy? You see what may be done by the Socratic and Platonic philosophers. Some of these allow such superiority to the goods of the mind, as quite to eclipse what concerns the body and all accidental circumstances. But others do not admit these to be goods; they repose all in the mind: whose disputes Carneades used, as an honorary arbitrator, to determine. For as what seemed goods to the Peripatetics, were allowed to be advantages by the Stoics: and as the Peripatetics allowed no more to riches, good health, and other things of that sort, than the Stoics; when these things were considered according to their reality, not by mere report; his opinion was, that there was no ground for disagreeing: therefore let the philosophers, that hold other tenets, see how they may carry this point. It is very agreeable to me that they make some professions worthy the mouth of a philosopher, with regard to a man's having always the means of living happily.

XLII. But as we are to depart in the morning, let us remember these five days' disputations, though indeed, I think, I shall write them: for how can I better employ the leisure I have, whatever it be owing to? and I will send these other five books to my Brutus; by whom I was not only incited to write on philosophy, but provoked. In which it is not easy to say what service I may be of to others; but in my own various and acute afflictions which surrounded me on all sides, I could find no better solace.

VINCENT, PRINTER, OXFORD.

Milton Keynes UK
Ingram Content Group UK Ltd.
UKHW020058040823
426310UK00005B/144

9 781015 611627